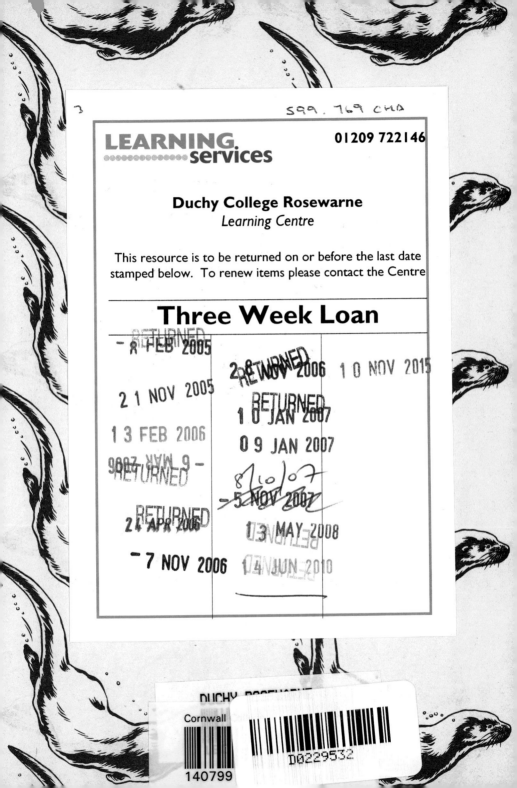

599. 769 CHA

3

OTTERS

OTTERS

•PAUL CHANIN•

with illustrations by
GUY TROUGHTON

Whittet Books

First published 1993
Text © 1993 by Paul Chanin
Illustrations © 1993 by Guy Troughton
Whittet Books Ltd, 18 Anley Road, London W14 0BY

Design by Richard Kelly

British Library Cataloguing-in-Publication Data. A catalogue record for this book is available from the British Library

ISBN 0 905483 90 1

Typeset by Litho Link Ltd, Welshpool, Powys, Wales
Printed and bound by WBC

Contents

Acknowledgments

I am writing this a few days after hearing that the Institute of Terrestrial Ecology's Research Station near Banchory has been destroyed by fire. Under the circumstances I have to start by paying tribute to the research on otters carried out there by Hans Kruuk, Jim Conroy and their colleagues over the past ten years or so. The hard work, ingenuity and sheer excellence of their work has transformed our view of the ecology of otters and ably demonstrates that worthwhile research can be done on an animal as elusive as the otter. I am also grateful to several members of the team, especially Jim Conroy, for talking to me about the research in progress while I was writing this book.

This is not to undervalue the work done by previous researchers, often working on their own or in small groups, who painstakingly pieced together much valuable information on the otter. I am particularly grateful to Sam Erlinge who guided my early interest and to Don Jefferies who has been a collaborator over many years. Thanks also to all others whose work has contributed to this book who, owing to the need to avoid littering the pages with references, have not necessarily been acknowledged in the text. My apologies to anyone who has been misquoted or misinterpreted.

I am extremely grateful to Su Hiscox, Jim Conroy and Don Jefferies for reading the book in draft. Their helpful comments enabled me to clarify the text and avoid a number of blunders. Needless to say, any mistakes or obscurities that remain are my own fault, probably where I ignored their advice.

Thanks are also due to Annabel Whittet for her patience over a much longer period than originally expected. Her low-key approach to recalcitrant authors is much appreciated.

Finally: Thank you, Sarah, this is for you.

What are otters?

Otters are members of the weasel family, the Mustelidae, one of seven families belonging to a group of mammals known as the Carnivora which includes wolves, dogs and foxes (the Canidae); bears (Ursidae); raccoons and pandas (Procyonidae); cats (Felidae); hyenas (Hyaenidae) and civets, genets and mongooses (Viverridae). Carnivores are typically meat-eaters with sharp canine teeth for killing and holding their prey and keen slicing cheek teeth for cutting up its flesh. On the other hand, their skeletons tend not to be specialized as many of them have to be very adaptable. Many can run quite quickly but also climb trees. Others need to be able to knock over or hold down struggling prey with their paws as well as run fast enough to catch it. The design of a carnivore's body is often therefore more of a compromise than, for example, a gazelle whose legs are highly adapted to running fast, or a gibbon whose long arms are beautifully designed for swinging through trees.

Mustelids fit this pattern rather well. They have long, thin bodies and short legs, ideal for pushing through dense undergrowth or hunting in

tunnels for prey, and can walk on the soles of their feet, like humans, rather than on their toes like the speedier cats, dogs and hyenas. However, their skulls are specialized, with an elongated cranium often topped by a narrow crest for the attachment of strong jaw muscles and sharp slicing molar teeth for turning prey into bite-sized chunks.

The Mustelidae are divided into five sub-families, the typical weasels (including stoats, polecats, mink, martens and the wolverine), the skunks, the badgers, the honey badger and of course, the otters.

There are several species of otters but at the moment there is no agreement as to how many. Until a few years ago it was generally accepted that there were 18 or 19, but now it is agreed that some of these are simply different varieties of the same species. Recently, an American zoologist recognized only 9 species and, for simplicity, I have used his arrangement, although other people prefer the classification used by two British taxonomists who recognized 13. If you want the full details you will have to turn to the books mentioned in the section on further reading (see p.125).

European otters
This is easy, there is only one, the subject of this book, our own species *Lutra lutra*, best described as the Eurasian otter. Although now missing

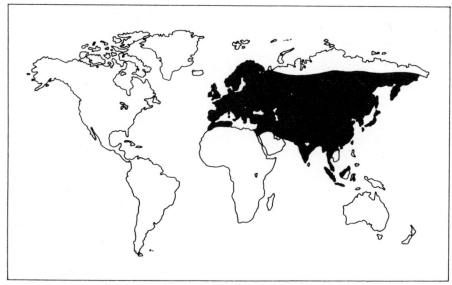

Distribution of the Eurasian otter.

from parts of its former range, it still inhabits an enormous area, much greater than any other species. As the map shows, its range extends from the cool, damp climate of the west of Ireland to the humid tropical forests of Asia and from the hot, dry lands of North Africa to the cold of northern Russia and Finland.

Asian otters

In addition to the Eurasian otter there are two species found in Asia, the smooth-coated otter (*Lutrogale perspicillata*) and the Asian (or Oriental) small-clawed otter (*Amblonyx cinerea*).

The small-clawed otter is a little smaller than the Eurasian otter (see p.12) and is probably one of the most familiar species since it is often kept in zoos and wildlife parks. In the wild, its diet consists of crabs, molluscs, frogs and small fish and, in keeping with this diet, which includes a high proportion of hard-shelled prey, its teeth are modified to be better at crushing than slicing. Another adaptation is reflected in its name. The claws are reduced to a vestige, with the result that the fore-paws look quite hand-like. In the wild they are used for probing in the mud and feeling under stones. In captivity, I have seen a tame one that was adept at juggling with hazel nuts and stealing key-rings from handbags. Another characteristic of this species is its sociability. Families are large (litters of 4 or 5 are normal) and may on occasion join together so that there have been sightings of as many as 15 in one group. It is found in south-east Asia, including parts of India and southern China.

The smooth-coated otter is similar in size and habits to the Eurasian otter. Little studied in the wild, it is probably best known from Gavin Maxwell's book, *Ring of Bright Water* (his first otter, Mijbil, was this species). Its diet consists principally of fish, although, like most otters, it does not disdain crabs in some areas. Smooth-coated otters have a very unusual distribution, the main part of the range covering India and south-east Asia but with an isolated population in the extensive marshes around the Tigris and Euphrates on the borders of Iran and Iraq.

African otters

South of the Sahara are two species, the clawless otter (*Aonyx capensis*) closely related to, but larger than the small-clawed, and the spotted-necked otter (*Hydrictis maculicollis*).

Clawless otters have lost their front claws entirely but retain those on the middle toes of the hind foot and, like their Asian cousins, specialize in invertebrate prey rather than in fish. In coastal regions they have even

been recorded as feeding on octopus. By contrast the smaller spotted-necked otter is a fish specialist.

Perhaps in connection with their diets, the two species are active at different times, the spotted-necked during the day and the clawless at dawn and dusk or at night. Both species are quite sociable and can often be seen in groups of 4 or 5 individuals. Occasionally spotted-necked otters have been seen in groups as large as 20.

American otters

There are two species of otter found in North America, the sea otter (*Enhydra lutris*, see below) and the North American river otter (*Lutra canadensis*). The river otter is generally put in the same genus as the Eurasian otter and the two species are very similar in most aspects of their biology. The most obvious difference is in reproduction: the American species has a very long gestation period due to a phenomenon known as delayed implantation.

Central and South America also have river otters in the genus *Lutra* and whether you consider there to be one species (the same one as in North

The giant otter of South America.

America) or several depends on which classification you prefer. In the table (see p.12), I have listed only one, but there is a case to be made for two additional species, one in Central and South America from Mexico to northern Argentina and the other in the far south, found only in Chile and southern Argentina.

Apart from the river otters, South America boasts two other distinct species. The giant otter (*Pteronura brasiliensis*), which can reach 1.8 m in length (about 6 ft), and the sea cat or marine otter (*Lutra felina*), one of the smallest species.

Giant otters are found mainly on larger rivers in northern and central South America where they live in family groups consisting of an adult male and female plus one or two litters of young. They feed primarily on fish, hunting close together in a group although probably not actually co-operating. Giant otters have been heavily hunted for fur in many parts of their former range, and are extinct in some.

Little is known of the sea cat, which lives on the west coast of South America in Peru and Chile. It lives beside the sea and feeds along the shore where it concentrates on invertebrate prey although there are reports of it venturing into rivers to catch freshwater shrimps. Fish are not ignored but only form a quarter of the prey taken.

The Pacific Ocean

Around much of the northern Pacific lives the intriguing sea otter, not to be confused with other otters that live beside the sea. Most species will probably venture out to sea from time to time and several, including our own, are capable of living along the coast. However these are merely inland otters living at the seaside, whereas the sea otter spends its entire life at sea. I could write a whole book on sea otters but unfortunately for me someone already has (see Further Information) so a potted history is all that is required.

Sea otters feed mainly on invertebrates and are particularly fond of sea urchins and abalones (large, limpet-like molluscs). They are renowned for their habit of using rocks as tools, both to acquire their prey (they use them to bludgeon abalones into letting go) and as anvils on which to crack open the shells of clams and mussels. Spending their whole lives at sea and rarely, if ever, venturing onto land, they need exceptionally good waterproofing and insulation. Evolution has provided this in one of the densest fur coats known. Unfortunately their luxuriant fur very nearly led to their downfall. Last century they were hunted almost to extinction for their pelts, but have been protected since 1911 and have recovered in parts

of their former range. Small populations are found off the West Coast of North America, the best known being in California. In the North Pacific they are found on the necklace of islands that connects America with Asia, consisting of the Alaskan Peninsula and the Aleutian Islands as well as the Kurile Islands which link Kamchatka to Japan.

Today they are well protected from exploitation but face, instead, other dangers. In March 1989 an oil spill from the super-tanker *Exxon Valdez* is known to have killed 1,000 of the 5,000 sea otters inhabiting the area round Prince William Sound in Alaska. How many died unseen will never be known.

Otters of the world

	Geographic range	Principal food	Approx. weight	Approx. length
Eurasian otter	Eur/Asia/Afr	Fish	8-10 kg (17-22 lb)	110-120 cm (43-47 in)
American river otter	N & S America	Fish	7-9 kg (15-19 lb)	110-120 cm (43-47 in)
Marine otter	S America	Inverts	4-5 kg (9-11 lb)	100-115 cm (39-45 in)
Smooth-coated otter	Asia	Fish	10-11 kg (22-24 lb)	110-130 cm (43-51 in)
Spotted-necked otter	Africa	Fish	5-6 kg (11-13 lb)	100-110 cm (39-43 in)
Asian small-clawed otter	Asia	Inverts	4-5 kg (9-11 lb)	65-95 cm (25-37 in)
African clawless otter	Africa	Inverts	18-20 kg (40-44 lb)	130-150 cm (51-59 in)
Giant otter	S America	Fish	26-32 kg (57-70 lb)	150-180 cm (59-71 in)
Sea otter	Pacific Ocean	Inverts	25-30 kg (55-66 lb)	130-140 cm (51-55 in)

Where possible, lengths and weights are given for males. Females are about 10 per cent shorter and 25 per cent lighter. For most species the tail is approximately one third of total length except for sea otter in which it is a quarter.

Where otters sleep

The places where otters rest or sleep have several names, some of which are derived from hunting terminology. Thus 'holt' usually refers to some sort of tunnel, and 'couches' are resting sites above ground. Hunters also talk about 'hovers' but I have never been

Spreading tree roots can provide good den sites.

entirely sure how these are defined. There is no single name that covers all the places that otters use, other than 'resting site' or 'den', but these usually imply an enclosed place.

One of the most comprehensive surveys of resting sites was made by Ian Coghill on the upper reaches of the Severn and its tributaries in Wales, where he recorded 256. These were all known to otter hunters and some had been used for periods of 20 to 40 years, while a few had been in use for 100 years or more. All of the sites were close to water, 90 per cent within 10 m (32 ft) of the bank (many actually on the river bank) and the remainder within 50 m (160 ft) of the water side.

His largest category was 'tree holts', all but one of which consisted of tunnels into or under the root systems. The odd one out was a hollow trunk. Over 90 per cent of these holts had entrances leading directly into deep water and nearly three-quarters were under trees which leaned out over the water. Ash and sycamore were the favourite species, having shallow-spreading root systems, ideal roofs for otter dens.

Trees also provide shelter when they or their branches get swept down river in spates and large tangles accumulate to form stick piles. Coghill recorded 34 of these which were used by otters in his study area, some lasting for surprisingly long periods of time (40 years was the maximum). The otters seemed to prefer those that formed over water rather than on land, particularly if the water was deep.

Just over 20 per cent of the resting sites were of more solid material – rock or concrete – and many of these were formed artificially. Three were natural rock cavities but the remainder were either drains or heaps of rock, forming embankments or created as spoil from quarries.

Fifty-one of the resting sites came into the category 'lying rough'. These were above ground, usually in thick vegetation such as reed-beds or osiers. They are probably even more common in low lying places where the water table is near the surface than in the upper reaches of the Severn. When otters were common in the Norfolk Broads they would often use couches in the reedbeds for breeding as well as for sleeping.

Coghill's final category was 'miscellaneous' and included rabbit burrows and badger setts together with one unique site – the back seat of a car, which was ending its days as bank protection on a Welsh river.

Where do otters live?

Otters are aquatic, or more correctly, semi-aquatic animals, which means that they spend much of their time, while active, in water. They find virtually all of their food in, on or beside water and their dens are usually close to water. However there are many different types of aquatic and waterside habitats, some of which are more suitable than others. Much depends on the availability of the resources needed to survive and breed. Needless to say, an important resource is food but otters also have to take into consideration the need for shelter and refuge, suitable breeding sites and of course potential mates. So, before looking at the habitats which could be exploited in Britain, it is a good idea to consider the essential resources in a little more detail.

Food is obviously fundamental and although otters may take other prey from time to time, occasionally in substantial amounts, in most places, for most of the time, fish form the bulk of their food. The actual diet is described in detail later but one consequence is clear: although the sparkling little upland streams of Dartmoor, Wales, the Pennines and Scotland are very attractive to people, they are of less benefit to otters because they are not very productive and do not have high densities of

Den in a grassy habitat.

fish. Large, productive lowland streams provide much more food which is present throughout the year and, other things being equal, are much better habitats.

What about resting sites, refuges and dens? In fact, in areas where they are unlikely to be disturbed directly by people, otters are not very choosy about where they sleep. Males in particular seem willing to lie up in places which can hardly be described as secure. In Shetland, they have been seen asleep on seashore rocks in broad daylight. Radio-tracking studies show that on some rivers otters may have very large numbers of sleeping sites to choose from and frequently change from one day to the next. One male used 27 sites during three months of tracking, 18 of which were above ground. These ranged from dense vegetation or substantial piles of sticks and branches to depressions in the bank-side where the plants were only 30 cm (12 in) high. Most of those below ground were natural holes under the roots of trees or amongst rocks and boulders although one was an old rabbit burrow. More than 90 per cent of the sites were within 50 m of the water and most of them within a few metres. Studies in Wales show that there, trees such as ash and sycamore with large root systems are important to otters as the roots are undermined by the water, forming hidden ledges and caverns.

Otters living on the west coast of Scotland and the Scottish islands seem to have little difficulty in finding holes and caverns amongst the rocks and they too can be very adaptable. I have tracked otters into sand dunes where I suspect they lie up in enlarged rabbit burrows, and they often burrow into the peat. Coastal otters generally seem to have fewer dens than those radio-tracked along rivers in eastern Scotland but it is not clear whether this is due to the fact that coastal otters have smaller home ranges or that there are fewer suitable dens available. Possibly both factors are significant.

Perhaps the most important choice lies with the female in finding a good breeding den, and some people believe that the lack of suitable sites may prevent them from breeding in certain areas. The problem, of course, is in knowing what makes a good breeding site. The radio-tracked otters revealed two dens with cubs, one of which was 40 m from the river and the other at least 100 m from the nearest stream. These, together with three breeding dens found by Rosemary Harper in other parts of Scotland, had one feature in common – they were extremely unlikely to be flooded. It is also interesting that two of the dens Rosemary found were well away from the main river although both were near or beside small streams of 0.5 m and 1.5 m in width. Clearly close proximity to a river is not essential

Some dens are amongst rocks.

for breeding dens and avoidance of flooding and the risk of disturbance might be more important in selection.

So, where *do* otters live? Well, they can be found living in freshwater, in estuaries and on the coast and, if it were not for the activities of man, they would probably be found in most freshwater, most estuaries and along much of the coast of Britain today. Man's influence is described in more detail later in the book; here I will simply try to explain the natural influences on otter distribution.

It is probably clear from what I have already said that there may be some places that could not support otters. Nevertheless throughout most of Britain and much of the rest of the otter's range even waterways that have little to offer the otter, tiny ponds or very small streams for example, are often close to or linked to more suitable habitat. This is why on the

Island of Coll, where the biggest stream is little more than 2 m (6 ft) wide, I found signs of otters throughout the island as well as on the coast. Tiny streams which had little food or shelter to offer the otter were used as routes through to the many lochs which are found inland. Tiny lochs, which might only have enough fish to support an otter for a short time, were also visited, though perhaps only occasionally; the otters would feed on trout and eels there when it was too rough to feed at sea.

Undoubtedly the best (optimal) freshwater habitat for otters is found along the large lowland streams of central and southern England. These are productive as well as being large and therefore have high densities of fish, particularly coarse fish. But here man has the greatest influence, as I will describe later (see p.113). I suspect that at one time, the best habitat in England was the Norfolk Broads. Not only were these extensive in area and highly productive but also very shallow, an important factor for otters when hunting. The lochs of the Scottish Highlands and the lakes of the Lake District have less to offer otters than those in the lowlands which are filled by water which has run off productive farmland rather than infertile hills. The seasons also play a part. For example, I have several times visited a small loch, about 600 m long and about a kilometre from the sea, on Islay in the Inner Hebrides. When we visited it in spring 1987 there were far more otter spraints (droppings) than we had ever seen before and practically all of them contained the remains of frogs. Presumably the otters had been there earlier in the year at spawning time, harvesting the frogs as they came to the waterside for their annual mating spree. This is one reason why marshes, fens and other wetlands which contain little open water are also valuable otter habitats.

Incidentally, large rivers are not always more productive than small. In northern Scotland on the rivers Dee and Don, otters spent more time hunting on the tributaries and small streams than the main river because the fishing was better there.

Similar considerations apply to the coast. Productive areas are best although it is probably also important for coastal otters to have places where they can feed when seas are rough. Although there are some fish to be found where the sea bed is sandy, the best hunting is undoubtedly around rocky areas where seaweeds can gain a foothold and provide shelter and food for large numbers of fish. It is easier for otters to catch food in shallow water than deep, so gently shelving rocky shores are ideal.

The extent to which otters used to live around the coasts of England is

Gulls waiting for scraps.

unrecorded but I suspect that they were widespread in suitable areas. In Cornwall, people still speak of the times when otters were regularly seen around the coast and even today it is sometimes possible to find spraints where small streams flow out into the sea. As recently as 1987, two friends of mine saw an otter just behind the public lavatories on Lamorna beach, between Penzance and Land's End, in broad daylight too. Similarly, the mud flats and marshes of north Norfolk bordering the Wash were used by otters at least into the 1980s. However it is Scotland that is best known for its coastal otters. Most of the west coast, the islands and part of the east coast are used by otters and it is to these areas that most people go when they want to see wild otters in Britain. The best habitat in Britain today may well be the east coast of the island of South Uist in the Outer Hebrides. Here there are a series of long finger-like sea lochs, some stretching 2 or 3 km (1-2 miles) inland from the open sea. Sheltered, shallow and with alternative prey available in the small freshwater lochs on the land between them, these seem to have a very high density of otters. Even so, you are not guaranteed a sight of an otter; I spent three days there a few years ago and did not spot a single one, though there were signs everywhere.

Signs of otters

One of the difficulties in studying shy and retiring animals like otters is just that – they are shy and retiring. In addition they are often nocturnal and usually scarce so it is hardly surprising that people studying them tend to spend more time looking for their signs than for the otters themselves. This is why the apparently arcane study of otter droppings, or spraints, is so important.

The significance of sprainting behaviour to otters is discussed in the chapter on communication but spraints are also of great interest to biologists, for two main reasons. The first is that they are a very good way of obtaining information about the otter's diet. Most food eaten by otters contains indigestible parts and these are eliminated in the faeces when they may be conveniently collected for study. The great advantage of using spraints in this way is that they are a constantly renewable source of material and this has enabled some people to collect a substantial amount of information on the diet of otters. Second, the fact that you can find otter spraint on a river is a clear indication that otters have been there, something which is otherwise very difficult to confirm. Unfortunately

Young otter sprainting.

counting otter spraints does not tell you how many otters there are in an area although it can give you a guide to the otter's distribution. There are several reasons for this. Unlike some animals (deer for example) which produce predictable numbers of roughly equal sized dung pellets each day, otters sometimes produce large spraints and sometimes smaller ones. In addition they do not necessarily leave all their spraints in places where you can find them. People have seen otters defaecating in water and even spraints on land are not necessarily accessible. Where people have been able to study otters over long periods they have found great changes in spraint numbers from month to month, and year to year which cannot be linked with changes in otter numbers. Some of the fluctuations can be explained by seasonal factors such as spraints being washed away by floods in winter and hard to find amongst dense vegetation in summer. Others may be linked to changes in behaviour, perhaps associated with breeding or territorial behaviour. The fact is however that we cannot yet make reliable predictions about numbers of otters from the numbers of their spraints.

Spraintology
The word spraint was originally used by hunters in the British Isles but has now passed into common use, at least amongst those interested in otters. The word is believed to come from the French *épreindre*, to squeeze out. The source of this information, *The Language of Field Sports* by C. E. Hare (who else?) includes about fifty words connected with otter hunting of which four are used for the otter's droppings ('spraint', 'wedging', 'coke' and, formerly, 'tredeles'). The origins of 'coke' I can understand as dried otter spraint does have some resemblance to the derivative of coal but, sadly, the origins of the others are not revealed. Zoologists often use the word 'scat' for faeces, particularly of carnivores, and 'scat' or 'spraint' can be used for otter droppings. However it is most important to remember that only otters produce spraints if you want to maintain your credibility with otter enthusiasts. You could get away with using the words 'coke' and 'wedging' in conversation with otter hunters but I have never heard 'tredeles' used and have no advice on how to pronounce it.

Otters have powerful digestions and only bones and fish scales pass right through the gut together with fur, feathers and the skeletons of insects or crayfish, depending on the otter's diet. The presence of fish bones in a scat, particularly the spiky vertebrae, is usually a good indication that you have found an otter spraint, although mink is also a possibility.

Scent seems to be important to otters for communication and spraints tend to be found in conspicuous places, sometimes in considerable numbers. The largest count I have heard of was of 250 spraints at one site. As spraint in the open tends to weather and disappear over a few weeks or months, such accumulations normally only occur in sheltered areas, under rocks and cliffs or in the entrance to dens.

Spraint sites seem, to humans at least, to be placed where other otters are most likely to encounter them. Conspicuous features of the river bank such as large rocks, the bases of bridges or large trees are often used while on the coast concentrations of spraints are found near dens, rolling places and freshwater pools. Where the soil is infertile, for example on the west coast of Scotland, otter spraints can often be easily located because the grass is particularly lush and green where it has been regularly fertilized.

Sometimes otters will scrape up sand, mud or even grass to form a small heap, usually called a 'sign heap' (see p.47) on which they deposit their spraint. At one time it was thought that these might have a special significance but I have found them mainly on smooth stretches of sand or mud; where there was nothing obvious to spraint on, the otter appeared to have con-

Spraints and scats

Otter spraints are not too difficult to find when you know where to look (assuming there are some otters present) but they can easily be confused at first with such things as twigs, leaves, moss and bird droppings. A close inspection will enable you to discard some of these fairly readily. Most bird droppings consist of very fine material which has been ground down in the gizzard and, although the appearance may be somewhat gritty, the particles are usually very fine. There is often some white material (uric acid) in bird droppings, though not always. A good indication that you have either an otter spraint or a mink scat is the presence of fish bones which are usually quite small (1-3 mm across) and are distinctly spiky.

A 'textbook' otter spraint is 6-8 cm long and about 1 cm in diameter, cylindrical and full of tiny spiky fish bones or scales. The colour is very variable, from black or dark greenish-brown to very pale grey, depending partly on age. A well weathered spraint can look like the result of leaving a cigar on

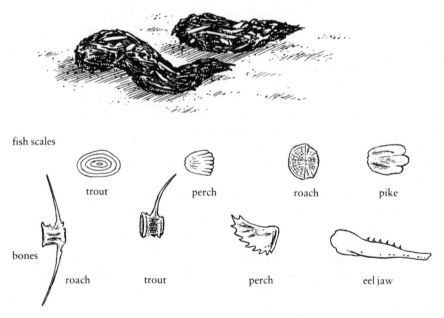

fish scales

trout   perch   roach   pike

bones

roach   trout   perch   eel jaw

Typical otter spraint (above) and typical contents (below).

an ash-tray to burn away undisturbed.

Needless to say textbook descriptions do not cover all eventualities and spraints can be much smaller than this as otters use them for communication (see later) and produce small spraints for marking purposes. Occasionally you will encounter no more than a tarry splodge, perhaps with a few fish bones in it. Fortunately the only likely source of confusion with otter spraint is mink scats and these are often quite distinctive. One of the best characteristics, at least in fresh specimens, is smell, since both species add a unique scent to their faeces from glands discharging into the rectum. Mink scats smell quite unpleasant when fresh although the odour fades over a few days. Otter spraints on the other hand have an inoffensive smell which is usually described as musky or musty, sometimes as fishy or spicy, and was once likened to the scent of laurel. C. E. Hare says, 'It is agreeably scented, like snuff.' My own view is that it is best described as 'ottery' amd the only way to learn it is to get someone else to show you a spraint.

There are also differences in appearance. Mink scats are smaller and thinner than the 'typical' otter spraints, perhaps 5-7 cm in length and about 7 mm in diameter. Usually tapering and sometimes twisted at the ends, they tend to be much more compact than spraints, which are rather loosely formed.

structed a spraint site for itself. One particularly industrious otter scraped up a total of 48 sign heaps around the shore of a small pool in south Devon during January of 1976. Most of these had a small spraint on top.

Otters are capable of quite remarkable feats of agility in using some spraint sites. More than once I have found spraint on horizontal branches only 15 cm or so in diameter, quite a balancing act. Another spraint site that I have seen was 3 m up in the branches of an old oak tree leaning over the River Wye. If Welsh otters are good climbers, Scottish otters seem to have good heads for heights; the most intriguing spraint site I have found was beside a freshwater pool at the top of a 45 m (150 ft) cliff in the Hebrides. The spraints were deposited only inches from a sheer drop to the sea below. It was certainly a loo with a view.

In contrast, people have sometimes seen otters sprainting in water and it has been suggested that this may be a special strategy adopted by females when they have young cubs. By not sprainting on land they may reduce the risks of predators finding and eating the cubs. Otter hunters certainly believed that females with cubs produced no scent.

Tracks and other signs

One can of course look for other signs of the presence of otters and the best alternative to spraints is footprints. Otters, like all mustelids, have five toes, whereas cats and dogs have only four. This means that if you have a clear print you only have to distinguish it from the tracks of mink, which are smaller, and badger, which are larger, to be sure that you are looking at an otter's footprint. Very occasionally, if you are lucky, you may find a print in soft mud in which the webs can be seen.

Needless to say, life is not always that kind. Very often you will find a nice patch of mud which has a confused mass of footprints, pitted by rain drops, trodden by people and dogs and with one or two faint prints at the edge which you hope might just be otter. Also, it is surprising how often you find 'four-toed' otters because the smallest toe does not make a mark, especially in firm mud or in sand. Even so, it may still be possible to recognize the prints perhaps by searching for one really good one. With experience you can distinguish a four-toed otter from a dog or fox print because the dog and fox both have very symmetrical prints whereas those of the otter are lopsided.

Although the best places to find footprints are usually at the waterside, on patches of mud or sand, otters also travel across land from time to time and sometimes make quite distinct trails. These are most easily seen in coastal areas where you find well worn paths connecting up dens,

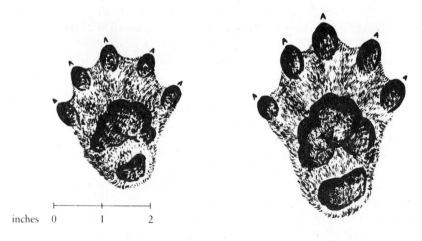

inches   0   1   2

The underside of an otter's right front foot (left) *and* (right) *hind foot.*

Sliding into the water.

freshwater pools and rolling places or around lakes where otters may take short cuts across peninsulas or have paths running to dens near the water. However, you can also find them near rivers, particularly those that meander a great deal. Otters will sometimes miss out a large loop in the river and run across the land to pick it up again. These trails are usually marked at intervals by spraints and, where there is a steep drop into the river, you may find a 'slide'.

Slides used to be thought of as otter playing places and it is possible that cubs may occasionally use them as such but those that I have seen have simply been where otters clamber up a steep bank out of the water or slip back in again. They remind me of the badger 'up-and-overs' we see on hedge banks in Devon. These are badger crossing places and get very worn by the regular passage of heavy badger feet but they are not used primarily for play.

The other signs of otters you may find are their dens (holts) and the remains of their meals. It can be quite difficult to distinguish between some otter dens and simple holes in the bank and since you should not disturb otter dens it is best not to search for them and, if you find one, to leave well alone. The best way of confirming that an otter uses such a hole is to find footprints or spraints beside it. It is rather similar with prey remains. Distinguishing between a fish that has been partially eaten by an otter and one that a mink has eaten is tricky. Again, the presence of footprints or spraints nearby is the best way to be sure. It is a little easier with coastal dens, particularly those under rocks or amongst boulders. They usually have a well worn path leading to them and much more spraint in or around the entrance.

Incidentally, country people, especially water bailiffs, tell stories about otters catching a whole salmon, taking 'one bite out of the shoulder' and leaving it on the bank, where of course, it can be collected by the bailiff and safely 'disposed of'. I am quite sure that this happened occasionally but perhaps not as often as is sometimes suggested and the bite out of the shoulder was probably a good deal more than that. One description suggested that the otter had eaten more than a pound of flesh. A very good meal for an otter but leaving plenty for the bailiff to consume since otters are known to have occasionally caught salmon up to 9 kg (20 lb) in weight!

Where can I see otters?

A frequent question and usually, I suspect, asked in the hope that I can recommend somewhere close to hand where you can easily pop down to the water side for a pleasant evening's otter watching. It is not that easy, at least, not in southern Britain where the question is usually asked.

In theory at least you ought to be able to see otters wherever they can be found, and, armed with the distribution map on page 110, you could head for the river bank and settle down to wait. I reckon that in most areas where otters are doing reasonably well, Wales and south-west England, for example, a fortnight of waiting twenty-four hours a day should normally be enough. In most places otters ought to pass you two or three times during that time. Not that you will see much though, unless you are very lucky, or have special equipment for night viewing; even then an otter could slip past without being noticed. Over a period of two years when I spent many nights otter watching on a lake where they passed the same spot on most nights, I never had more than a brief glimpse: sometimes a V-shaped wake as the otter swam under the bridge; once or twice a ghostly humped back on the far bank as it went to its spraint site; on one very bright night I had a really clear view as one swam towards me, dived as it came close to the bridge I was sitting beside, and then swam underwater past me, just visible through my binoculars. A few people have become successful otter watchers in southern parts of Britain but it needs a tremendous amount of persistence in the face of a very high proportion of unsuccessful nights. An ability to do without sleep is a great asset not to mention an understanding employer, or at least an occupation you can carry out on autopilot.

On the whole, in southern Britain, I have always recommended the enthusiastic otter spotter to take up badger watching, it's much more productive. Badgers are a great deal more common than otters and are found more or less throughout Britian; they are reasonably predictable, usually coming out of the same hole each night at about the same time; and they have nice stripy faces to help you see them in the half dark. Much simpler and just as exciting.

Alternatively of course you could move to Scotland, preferably the west coast or one of the islands. Not only are otters more abundant in good coastal habitats than in less productive freshwater ones but they are also much more likely to come out during the day.

The V shaped wake.

The best technique for seeing otters in Scotland seems to be to make sure I am not with you when you are looking for them. Many times people have seen them just before or just after I have visited a place and there are countless spots where I have been assured, 'You are certain to see otters there,' but have failed to do so. More practically, the best thing to do is to walk quietly and keep scanning the water surface and shoreline. Binoculars are usually essential, not least for eliminating the numerous otter-like things you will see, seals and fronds of kelp in particular. (I once spent ten minutes carefully scrutinizing a hooded crow that was pretending to be an otter.) Sooner or later, though, you will be lucky and may have a very rewarding experience. Once, for example, after we had been watching one otter feeding on a Scottish sea loch for about half an hour, it disappeared. After ten minutes we got up to continue our walk only to find two more padding down the beach towards us. Whether these were dim, over-confident or just short-sighted I don't know, but they ambled down to the water's edge about 50 m away from three humans and two dogs and proceeded to fish in full view for about 45 minutes.

Apart from keeping quiet and being watchful, I don't believe there are any other rules for otter watching in coastal areas. It is obviously well worth listening to locals who will often know of places where they may be seen but I suspect you will be just as likely, perhaps even more likely, to find them elsewhere, off the beaten track where people do not go very often. On my last visit to the Hebrides, we saw otters four times in a week. I must be getting better at it.

For inland waters I have two further tips. One is to take up fishing. I think I have had more reports of otter sightings from people who go night fishing for sea-trout than any other single activity. I have also heard of one unfortunate otter which was disturbed from his daytime slumber by the activities of biologists studying fish in the River Otter in east Devon. The otter dived into the stream to escape, not realizing that they were using electric fishing equipment. It must have been a stunning experience; I understand it broke the world record for diving into a river and straight back out again.

The other suggestion is to take up bird-watching and to visit the RSPB's reserve at Leighton Moss in Lancashire. There are a number of hides at this reserve from which otters are frequently seen and, even if you don't spot one, there are plenty of fascinating birds to watch.

Finally of course, there are otters in a number of zoos, although these are not usually the Eurasian species (Asian small-clawed are most common). The best places to see Eurasian otters are at the Otter Trust which now has two sites, one at Earsham on the Norfolk/Suffolk border and the other in north Cornwall, near Launceston. Otters breed at both places; at Earsham particularly you can compare ours with other species.

Size, shape and appearance

With its distinctive hump-backed gait, short legs, long neck, body and tail, the otter is quite distinctive when seen in the open in broad daylight. However, it is surprising how often otters are confused with other animals, particularly mink but also on one occasion water voles. Very often this is due to lack of knowledge and experience. A colleague who travelled with great excitement to a Midland river where otters had confidently, but surprisingly, been identified was somewhat disillusioned when she was proudly shown water voles, some thirty times smaller than a female otter! However it must be said that sightings are frequently not under ideal conditions and I have been fooled when what I thought was an otter swimming across a pool turned out to be a mink. Most embarrassing, since I was radio-tracking the mink at the time.

cat

otter

mink

Mink, otter and a fairly large cat.

Another possible source of confusion around the coast is seals. It is easy to be confused, particularly if the animal is not close and the sea is a little choppy. But seals are much larger than otters and, when seen close to, their relatively larger eyes and narrower muzzles are obvious. Seals also tend to rest vertically in the water with only their noses or heads showing whereas otters more often lie horizontally with their backs and sometimes their tails at the surface. You might think that you would be safe on a river, but beware. Seals do venture quite long distances inland, and have

reached as far as St Ives on the River Ouse for example, over 60 km (38 miles) from the Wash as the crow flies and rather more as the seal swims.

The comparisons in the table should help in recognizing an otter and distinguishing it from the animal it is most likely to be confused with, the mink.

Comparison of mink and otter

	Mink	Otter
Size	Smaller than the average cat.	Larger than the largest cat.
Colour	Dark brown, almost black but occasionally occurs in unusual colours because of ancestry on fur farms. Silver grey or blue grey is most common but yellowish brown or white occasionally occurs.	Mid brown when dry but may appear much darker when wet. After shaking the coat may have a spiky appearance.
Patterns	Underside same colour as back but distinct white spots may be visible under chin (may also be on chest and abdomen).	Underside usually paler than back. May be white or cream patch under chin but not distinct.
Shape	Pointed face, thinner than a dachshund.	Flattened wedge-shaped head with broad whiskery muzzle. More stretched corgi than dachshund in shape.
Tail	Bushy and cylindrical like a cat's tail. Half the length of the body.	Stout at the base, tapering to a point. About 40 per cent of body length.
Behaviour	Curious and apparently unafraid of humans. Often hunts by diving into water from bank, rock or log. Regularly seen in daylight.	Shy and retiring, usually avoids humans. Hunts by diving repeatedly in same area from surface of the water. Rarely seen in daylight except in remote, usually coastal areas.

Living in water

Living, or even just hunting, in water presents many problems that land animals do not have to face. In particular, water is cold, dense and lacks oxygen. There are ways to overcome all these difficulties and if you look closely at whales, dolphins and seals, you can soon recognize many of them. Thus they all have a torpedo-shaped body and smooth skin so that they can slip easily through the water (no sharp projections like shoulders to create drag). Flipper-like feet provide good propulsion in water and plenty of blubber helps to smooth the edges and keep the warmth in. The

Otters are well adapted to life in water . . .

. . . but swimming has to be practised.

trick that the otter has had to accomplish is how to be sufficiently good at living in water to be able to catch fish in their natural element, while being reasonably proficient at moving on land, where it still spends much of its time.

It is no coincidence then that the long sinuous body of a typical mustelid seems to be well adapted for an aquatic life. Swimming for their supper has evolved at least twice in the family (otters and mink) and both whales and seals had long-bodied, otter-like ancestors. Since otters spend a lot of time out of water, it is not surprising that the body shape of the semi-aquatic otter is very similar to its terrestrial cousins such as polecat and pine marten. Apart perhaps from the stout tail and slightly over-sized feet, one would be hard put to find any characteristic of the otter's skeleton or skull that pointed to its aquatic way of life. It is only when you begin to look at the soft parts that you find the subtle, but important differences between otters and their close relatives which are due to their aquatic habits.

Perhaps the most obvious feature is the webbing on an otter's feet. This extends for much of the length of each digit although not to the very end. It is not unique – dogs have distinct, though less extensive, webs between their toes – but, not surprisingly, the otter has developed them much further. The paws are also a little larger than one might expect, probably

to provide a bit more push when swimming. Incidentally this is carried to extremes in the two largest species, giant otters and sea otters, which look as if they are wearing clown's boots on their hind feet.

The otter's tail is stout at the base and tapers towards the tip where it is noticeably flattened. Although it was sometimes called the rudder by otter hunters, it is not flattened from side to side but from top to bottom because it forms part of the propulsion unit when swimming fast underwater (see p.42 locomotion).

Keeping warm and dry is important to otters and, like many other mammals, their fur consists of two types of hair, stout guard hairs which may be up to 20 mm long and form a waterproof outer covering, plus a denser, finer layer of underfur which constitutes the otter's thermal underwear. Because they have to spend so much time in water, otters have developed an extremely thick coat (which is why their skins used to be prized in the fur trade). A Canadian scientist once counted the hairs on patches of otter skin and concluded that there were about 60,000 per square centimetre (not far short of 400,000 per square inch). The fur must be kept in good condition and grooming is a very important part of otter life. It has recently been shown that sea water tends to reduce the waterproofing qualities of otter fur and this is why freshwater pools are so important to otters living on the coast. When they have finished swimming they wash the salt off in the pools and then squirm on the ground nearby to rub themselves dry against the vegetation. If they are unable to wash in fresh water, salt crystals begin to form in the fur and the guard hairs clump together. The fur becomes lifeless and loses its normal fluffy appearance as well as its insulating properties in the water.

Another aid to keeping warm is to have a high metabolic rate. All mammals are able to adjust their metabolisms to circumstances and have various ways of maintaining their bodies at a constant temperature. Small mammals, like shrews, have a relatively large surface area and lose heat quickly, so they have a high metabolic rate, while large ones like elephants can afford to tick over more slowly. If you compare otters with similarly sized animals that do not hunt in water you find that their metabolism is about 20 per cent higher to compensate for the fact that they lose heat more rapidly in water than in air. Despite this they can still get chilled if they stay in water too long, particularly if they are hunting in deeper water where the air is squeezed out of their fur more quickly. Coastal otters will only fish for fifteen minutes or so before coming ashore to groom, rest and warm up.

Otter senses

Semi-aquatic animals like otters have to face entirely different sensory problems in the two media in which they live. The properties of air and water being so different, senses that work well in one may be much less effective in the other. A simple example is the sense of smell. Noses work very well in air. Each breath sucks past the sensory organs a large sample of air in which various compounds, present in minute quantities, can be detected, analysed and often identified. Of course, the air is on its way down to the lungs where it has an important role to play in respiration, so any attempt to sample water using the same process would have catastrophic consequences; because the mammalian nose is used for breathing as well as smelling, sniffing in water is not a good idea.

There has been a suggestion that otters might be able to use the sensitive skin around their nostrils to 'taste' underwater but there is, as yet, no proof of this. Nevertheless, scent does have an important part to play in their lives, far greater than for humans. This should not be too surprising since otters spend more of their time out of the water than in it and much

Grooming – the final touches.

Still wet from swimming.

activity takes place on land. Like carnivores, they undoubtedly use scent for hunting on land, even if they cannot in water. Scent also plays an important role in communication and probably in detecting danger as well. No one has tested the sensitivity of the otter nose but it seems likely that it is similar to other carnivores like dogs.

Otters' eyes are not very large and compared to humans they seem to be quite short-sighted on land but their vision is certainly adequate at short distances. When light passes from one medium into another (from air to water or from either to glass) the rays are bent. You can see this if you hold a pencil or stick half in water; it appears to bend at the junction. This property (refraction) is of enormous benefit to mankind because it allows us to manufacture lenses. Without refraction there would be no microscopes, no binoculars, no cameras; come to that no eyes either, at least not like the ones we have now. However, because the degree of bending varies depending on which of the two media the light is passing between, eyes that are adapted to see in air have major problems in focusing in water. Humans overcome this problem by putting a layer of air (and glass) between the surface of the eye and water but otters have overcome the same problem without resorting to goggles. In clear water and bright light otters can focus and resolve fine detail as well as in air because they can modify the shape of the lens in the eye to make it more spherical. So on a bright sunny day in a clear moorland stream otters are able to hunt by sight. Unfortunately they often have to hunt in murky water and on dark nights, yet they still manage to catch fish. How do they do it?

Small eyes and ears but very large whiskers.

A simple but elegant series of experiments by Jim Green showed how. He timed two captive otters catching fish in a clear pool and then again in the same pool after he had tipped in a quantity of powdered charcoal. This made the water so dark that a shiny metal object could only be seen if it was less than 10 cm (4 in) from the surface. Both otters took four times longer to catch fish in the dark than in clear water. One of the otters was then given a trim. The long whiskers (vibrissae) growing around his muzzle were all cut back (they grew again afterwards). In clear water he was just as successful at catching fish as before but this time, in the darkened water, he took twenty times as long. So it seems that the vibrissae are used to detect the presence of fish when otters are unable to use their eyes. Rather than feel the fish direct, the whiskers probably detect the regular vibrations caused by the beat of the fish's tail as it swims away from the otter. Interestingly, studies of the otter's brain have shown that the area that deals with signals coming in from the facial area is larger than normal in river otters and giant otters. Sea otters and clawless otters by contrast have an enlarged area dealing with information coming from their sensitive fore-paws.

Otters' ears are tiny but this is probably more in the interests of streamlining than because they are unimportant. Indeed otters seem to have quite sensitive hearing, much better than ours, and Philip Wayre has suggested that they can respond to sounds inaudible to humans. Once again, this is fine on land but different in the water. Water transmits sound very well, far better than air but this turns out to be a disadvantage in some ways. The problem is that, although you can hear sounds well underwater, it is almost impossible to determine which way they are coming from unless you have special modifications to the parts of the ear within the head. Otters do not have these adaptions (although dolphins do) so it seems unlikely that they use sound for locating prey under water. Incidentally, you may think that fish do not make much noise so sound would not be any good for finding them. This may well be the case but you should remember that, like bats, some whales and possibly some seals use echo-location to find their prey.

So, to summarize: in air, sound, scent and sight are the most important senses, in that order; below the surface of the water, sight and feel are used.

Locomotion

Otters are not the most graceful of creatures on land. They don't quite waddle but their hump-backed gait is not the most elegant means of locomotion. Nor are they particularly fast movers, but this is hardly surprising given their short legs and flat-footed stance. Walking is the preferred means of getting about but, if pressed, an otter will break into a run or a bounding gallop. It has been claimed that the American river otter can run as fast as a man but this probably depends on the circumstances. On the flat a man would undoubtedly be able to outpace an otter but Jim Conroy finds that it is not so easy along the river bank, especially if you are carrying a typical field biologist's equipment such as radio-receiver, antenna, notebooks, night viewer and so on. I know of no one who has timed a Eurasian otter on land, but a spotted-necked otter was timed at 1.4 metres per second (3.3 mph) when running and 2 metres per second (4.5 mph) when galloping, not much more than a vigorous walk for a human.

When otters make substantial journeys, they usually do so in the water, travelling at the surface, although occasional short cuts may be made across land, at large meanders for example, when visiting isolated lakes or crossing watersheds. Considerable distances can be covered; Don Jefferies once followed an otter swimming down a Suffolk river for nearly 8 hours, during which it covered 11 km (over 7 miles), a speed of about 0.4 metres per second (just under 1 mph).

In water of course they are much more at home. Swimming at the surface is accomplished by a sort of dog-paddle using all four legs. Interestingly there seems to be no fixed pattern to this. Rather than using the typical walking pattern of most mammals, otters adopt a more casual approach sometimes kicking all four legs alternately, sometimes with two from the same side or two from the same end. They may even thrust with all four together. The same applies underwater when swimming slowly but if the otter needs to accelerate it kicks with the hind legs together. As it does so the back undulates up and down so that the hind end of the body, including the tail, functions as a unit providing a powerful thrust. While swimming in a straight line, it tucks its fore-paws into its chest, bringing them into action for steering. Otters are not averse to getting a bit of extra push off the bottom, either with the front legs in steering or with the back to gain speed. Film of otters swimming often shows them using boulders,

Coming up . . .

Going down . . .

The Loch Ness monster?

submerged logs or the bottom in this way and sometimes they can give the game away by pushing off the side of an artificial pool which has been made to look like natural habitat.

Although otters are clearly much more graceful in water than on land, they do not move as quickly. The spotted-necked otter mentioned above achieved speeds of 1.1 metres per second (2.5 mph) in water and it has been estimated that the Eurasian otters swim at about that speed underwater.

Of course all this vigorous exercise uses up oxygen and the size of the otter has a major influence on the length of time it can stay submerged. Large animals can hold their breaths for very much longer than small ones so you might expect that otters would normally dive for quite short times compared to humans. Nevertheless people are often surprised to find that otter dives are usually less than 30 seconds and that dives in excess of 45 seconds are very rare. *In extremis* otters can probably survive for about 3 minutes before drowning.

Otters normally dive from the surface of the water and probably only launch themselves from the bank when frightened. The surface dive is quite distinctive with the back forming a graceful arch and the hind legs and tail following it down into the water. This rolling dive is not unlike that used by large whales and seems to help drive the animal down into the water, an important benefit since otters usually hunt near the bottom. When they are swimming rapidly near the surface they use a series of shallow dives, breaking the surface every ten metres or so.

Communication

Eurasian otters are not particularly sociable animals and if you see a small group, the chances are that it is a family, consisting of the female with her young, or the young on their own. Two otters together may sometimes be a breeding pair but, since courtship lasts only a few days before the sexes separate, this is less likely. The more sociable otters, such as Asian small-clawed and giant otters, have quite a repertoire of calls and chatter noisily to one another but the lonely Eurasian otter is not a particularly vocal animal. Philip Wayre has had more opportunity to get to know their language than most as he has bred otters many times and hand-reared several. He recognizes three main types of call.

The first is the famous otter's whistle, actually a high-pitched squeak which is mainly used for keeping contact. Philip Wayre translates it as, 'I'm here. Where are you?' It carries quite a way and is the sound most people associate with otters. (Incidentally, hearing a whistle on the river bank at night does not necessarily mean an otter. I am afraid there is a whole range of animals along the waterside whistling and squeaking away pretending to be otters, so it is not a reliable clue.) A quieter call, the 'hah' sound, is used by females to warn cubs of danger but it may also be used at times of unease or when an animal is startled or frightened. It sounds like a sharp exhalation of breath.

Then there are a number of more complex noises variously described as chittering, chuckling, whickering and twittering. The exact nature depends on the circumstances. High-pitched calls indicate annoyance or threat while quieter, lower tones are used in greeting. Cubs make twittering noises when they are very young perhaps to indicate to the female that they are hungry. Otters are noisiest of all when mating but there is no agreement on how to describe the sounds that are used: 'chirruping', 'purring', 'yarring' come from one report and 'harsh purring, staccato grunts and squeaks' from another. No doubt the otters understand what it all means.

It is equally difficult for humans to understand the exact meanings in another important form of communication between otters, scent, although some attempts have been made to find out at least what sort of information might be passed on. Most attention has been paid to the anal glands which discharge a rich cocktail of chemicals into the rectum and thereby taint the otter's faeces. This is what gives spraint its distinctive smell and, while people sometimes describe it as being fishy, this has nothing to do with the diet, spraints containing only mammal remains smell exactly the same. Chemical analysis of the contents shows that although all spraints smell similar (to humans) there are differences between the scent of one otter and another. However, the scent 'profile' of one otter remains constant over periods of several weeks. One compound seems to be present in quite large quantities and this may be the one that humans notice and that gives the characteristic 'ottery' odour to spraints. Others are much more variable in quantity and might be used to distinguish individuality. As far as we know there is no indication of the sex of the animal in its scent but it seems quite likely that otters can tell how recently the spraint was deposited because the various constituents evaporate at different rates. Just as with Chanel No. 5, fresh scent is quite different from stale. Males seem to travel round their ranges, refreshing the scent marks ever few days; when they do not it seems to take less than a week for other otters to realize it is no longer happening (see below).

Experiments with captive otters show that they are able to recognize the scents of individuals although we still do not know exactly how this information might be used in the wild. Nevertheless it is obvious that scent communication plays a very important part in otters' lives because of the amount of time they invest in it. Not only do they take the trouble to leave their spraints where other otters are likely to find them but they also spend quite a lot of time investigating those they find at each spraint site before turning round and depositing another addition to the bulletin-board.

Typical spraint site.

Where good spraint sites are scarce, otters may make sign heaps.

In a very careful study of the distribution of spraint sites on the west coast of Scotland, Beverly Trowbridge found that spraints were clumped around potential dens, resting sites and freshwater pools. These 'spraint stations' were spread along the coast so that otters coming ashore from the sea were likely to come across one very quickly. Where there were trails heading inland, often beside small streams, spraints were distributed at random but, with a density of twenty per kilometre, any otter following a trail would be likely to encounter a spraint very soon.

So, what is the scent for? The answer is that we don't really know. It was once said that is was used as a territory marker and certainly in areas where otters are strongly territorial there is evidence that it has an important role to play. The best evidence comes from Sweden where Sam Erlinge observed that when a male died, its territory was taken over within a week by a male from a neighbouring, less desirable territory, despite the fact that up to that time it had never been known to venture beyond a narrow zone of overlap between the territories. Even so, although neighbours may not intrude too far, it is quite clear that itinerant otters do enter the territories of residents, so scent cannot simply be a warning to keep out. A current theory suggests that it may enable trespassers to know when they have met the territory owner. If they encounter an otter which smells the same as most of the spraints in the area, it must be the resident. Since only big strong otters are likely to be territory holders it is probably a good idea to avoid confrontation and keep out the way. The intruder gains by avoiding a fight with a potentially superior rival and the resident by demonstrating its superiority in an indirect manner rather than a costly and risky show of force.

This argument breaks down somewhat in areas where otters are not strictly territorial and their home ranges overlap substantially, unless of course the residents tolerate each other in their home ranges but not intruders. It is also hard to reconcile with an observation made by Jim and Rosemary Green. They were able to mark the spraints of their female otters and showed that only a small proportion of the spraints in their home ranges were produced by the females themselves. They marked at a much lower rate than the adult male in a nearby area, suggesting a difference in marking behaviour between the sexes. There is obviously still a lot to learn about the significance of scent marking in otters.

Many mammals have more than one type of scent gland, indeed some have a positive armoury. However, apart from the anal glands, the only other source of scent that has been seriously considered in otters is urine. Male otters do not use urine to scent mark in the way that domestic dogs do but it is possible that there are compounds in the urine of female otters in breeding condition which would have the same effect as that of female dogs in season, a powerful attractant to the opposite sex! The chances of stumbling across a female in oestrous would be greatly enhanced if she were able to leave an odorous message in her range signalling her availability.

In order to investigate this, Beverly Trowbridge managed to collect regular samples of the urine of a captive female otter by concealing a suitable receptacle under a layer of sand where the otter normally urinated. However, chemical analyses of the urine, although revealing changes in concentrations of hormones over time did not show any clear evidence that they could be linked with the oestrous cycle.

Finding and catching prey

Like all good carnivores, otters adapt their hunting behaviour to circumstances and the techniques for catching fish, frogs, rabbits and ducks are naturally very different. Needless to say most observations of otter hunting behaviour are limited to the time spent on the surface between dives and there are very few reports of what happens underwater or when otters hunt other animals. Once again you have to piece together information from captive animals with snippets of information from the wild.

It seems that otters hunting fish probably use sight to find them where the water is reasonably clear but in dark or turbid water they have to rely

Small prey are consumed in the water.

on their whiskers detecting the beat of a fish's tail. In still water, fish which do not move might be safe but the disturbance caused by the otter's searching may well be enough to put a fish to flight and thereby let the otter know it is there. In running water fish would need to swim just to keep still but whether otters would be able to distinguish the beat of a fishy tail from the turbulence of water tumbling over rocks we do not know. The river would no doubt produce greater vibrations but perhaps the regularity of the tail-beat would help the otter. Otters seem to forage under stones and amongst weed in order to try and flush out their prey. In Shetland they hunt mainly on the bottom and spend more time feeding in areas where the beds of seaweed are patchy and have longer 'edges' than in solid masses of kelp. When the water is too shallow to swim, an otter can still manage to find prey by walking along the bottom with its head under water using its nose to turn over stones. This method works well for crayfish and slow moving species but a medium sized fish would probably find it easier to get away where it can swim but the otter cannot.

Captive otters in clear pools seem to hunt fish from below, perhaps because it is harder for the fish to detect them that way or perhaps because it is easier for the otter to see the fish. No one knows how many chases end in failure in the wild but Philip Wayre found that if the fish managed to get more than 2 or 3 m ahead it was safe, at least for the time being. In fact it is quite remarkable that otters can catch some species of fish at all because fish have tremendous acceleration. A 25 cm (10 in) trout can travel about 2 m in the first second of flight but it quickly tires and over a period of 10 seconds its average speed would come much closer to that of the otter. Indeed the otter's main strategy with fast swimming fish is probably to try and tire them out by chasing them persistently. In fairly shallow water this is not too difficult and hunting otters seem to be able to snatch a quick gulp of air at the surface without pausing in their pursuit. In deeper water however the otter has to return to the surface every so often to breathe and this gives its quarry ample time to escape or hide. This is probably why otters hunting in the sea concentrate mainly on slower swimming flatfish and other bottom-dwelling species.

In fact the need to breathe must severely restrict the depth of water in which otters can fish, at least for bottom-living species. In water 10 m (32 ft) deep an otter might need to spend as much as 20 seconds in travelling from the surface to the bottom and back again, which does not leave much time for hunting. This probably explains why in Shetland Hans Kruuk found that nearly two-thirds of dives were in water less than 3 m (9 ft) deep, even though this made up less than a quarter of the area easily available to them and otters were sometimes seen to hunt in water up to 14 m (46 ft) deep. The tidal range in Shetland is not very great but even so the otters hunted less at high tide than at other times. Elsewhere the state of the tide could be even more important in determining when otters feed.

Once the otter gets close enough, it will grab the fish in its jaws, although sometimes the front paws are used as well. Small fish are eaten at the surface so that the otter can quickly resume hunting but larger specimens are carried to the shore and consumed at the waterside. Captive otters will sometimes 'play' with their food, especially eels, which are not easily killed, but whether this happens much in the wild is unclear.

Not every dive is successful of course, many end with the otter returning to the surface empty handed, or at least empty mouthed. Around the coast otters come up with prey on a quarter to a third of their dives but otters hunting on a freshwater loch 2 or 3 m deep only caught prey on 1 out of 14 dives. However the freshwater prey were rather larger than the marine. Most were eels between 300 and 500 g (10 to 17 oz) in weight compared to the butterfish, blennies and sea scorpions on the coast, less than a sixth of which weighed more than 100 g (3.5 oz). Three large eels would probably satisfy an otter's needs for one day but it would need far more of the smaller marine fish to do so.

For other types of prey there are even fewer observations. Otters will sometimes catch water-birds by swimming under them and grabbing them from below but I suspect that most are caught while nesting or roosting. Terrestrial prey does not form a major part of the diet and it seems unlikely that otters would hunt small mammals such as mice, rats and voles deliberately although they would undoubtedly kill one if they could get close enough. Rabbits are the species most likely to attract the attention of otters because they often live in large colonies and each one would provide a substantial meal. However, an otter would probably be unable to catch a fit rabbit unless it were taken unawares. Perhaps otters stalk them and then pounce or they may have to concentrate on very young rabbits or those that are less fit and agile.

Frogs require another hunting strategy and since most are taken either during the spawning or the hibernation period there may even be two strategies. They can be so numerous at spawning sites that one imagines that otters can walk along practically grazing on them at the water's edge. During hibernation the frogs hide in the mud at the bottom of small bodies of water when otters must search for them by feel.

What do otters eat?

There are no prizes for answering 'Otters eat fish,' but possibly a consolation prize for following up the answer with further questions such as, 'What sort of fish do they eat?' 'What else do they eat?' 'How much do they eat?' All these questions interest ecologists and some of them interest fishermen as well, so it is not surprising that a great deal of effort has been put into studying the diet of otters.

In order to answer questions like these you need to have suitable techniques for studying the diet and there are three available, each with its own advantages and disadvantages: direct observation, gut content analysis and spraint analysis.

There is a great deal of anecdotal evidence about what otters eat, based on observations of them catching or eating fish, but the problem is that people are much more likely to notice, and make a note of, otters eating large or valuable fish such as salmon and trout than small but possibly more frequently eaten ones like eels or sticklebacks. As otters are largely nocturnal throughout much of Britain the only substantial body of data on their diet based on direct observations comes from the coasts of

Eels are a favoured food.

Scotland, particularly Shetland. Here, over a period of four years, Hans Kruuk and his colleagues observed 13,300 otter dives which resulted in 3,585 prey captures. They were able to identify 58 per cent of the prey and also to estimate the length of the prey by comparison with the size of the otter's head. This could then be converted to weight of prey consumed.

Analysis of the contents of guts is a messy business but it can be fairly easy to identify the size and type of prey if digestion has not proceeded far. The biggest problem is that you have to have dead otters, and so this technique has only successfully been used in areas where otters have been hunted for their fur, such as North America, Scandinavia and Russia. As hunting for fur is seasonal (the fur is best in winter) and otters are killed over a wide area, it has limited value even there.

By contrast, spraints are reasonably easy to collect and are, effectively, a renewable resource. Collecting them does not harm individual otters and it is possible to build up large collections by regular and diligent searching. For example, over a period of two years, Sam Erlinge collected 15,000 in various parts of Sweden, giving him a very detailed picture of the diet in different areas and throughout the year.

Spraints contain the indigestible remains of recent meals and, provided you can recognize the fragments, it is very easy to work out what the otters have been eating. It is less simple, however, to determine the relative quantities. Since fish do indeed form the bulk of the diet, the first need when studying otters' diet is to collect samples of fish from the locality, remove the flesh and make a collection of representative bones. Vertebrae and scales are the most frequently encountered remains but various other typical bones can also be added to the reference collection. It is then a simple matter (in theory at least) to compare the fragments in the spraint with those in the collection. In practice, there are always many bits which are impossible to identify and generally speaking the fewer species of fish available to otters, the fewer unidentifiable remains you will be left with, because there is less opportunity for confusion. A key to remains in otter spraints has been published by the Mammal Society, which works reasonably well in some areas of the country, but it does not include every species of freshwater fish and none of the marine ones. There are also keys available for the identification of hair and feathers.

Once you have identified the remains, you still have to quantify your findings and this is less straightforward. Some prey will have a very high ratio of indigestible matter to meat, crabs and crayfish for example, while others will produce few remains in the spraint. Even similar types of prey contribute differently to the spraint contents, eels for example contain about half as much indigestible matter as trout. There are various ways to overcome this, using so-called 'correction factors', calculated to enable you to estimate the original proportions of different prey in the diet. In practice they are time-consuming to use and most people use a simple formula based on the number of times a particular type of prey occurs in the spraints. This can lead to an overestimation of the importance of small prey such as sticklebacks if they are eaten regularly or of prey with a high proportion of indigestible remains such as crayfish or crabs. However, provided this is borne in mind 'frequency of occurrence' gives a useful guide to the diet.

What sort of fish?
Otters living in freshwater generally take whatever fish are most readily available, whether they be sticklebacks, trout, roach, perch or eels. However, where there is a choice, there seems to be a tendency for them to take disproportionate numbers of certain types of fish, particularly those that are easier to catch. On the whole they will concentrate on the slower swimming coarse fish, particularly eels if they can. However in many diets this is not possible and on the Dartmoor streams where I first studied otter diets, 60 per cent of the remains in spraint were salmonid fish, mainly trout and salmon parr. On the other hand, a further 30 per cent were eels, despite the fact that they were quite scarce in the river. Several hundred miles away, in a loch in north-east Scotland, David Jenkins and his colleagues found that eels were the most frequently eaten item for much of the year, usually occurring in more than 85 per cent of spraints each month.

Some species seem to be overlooked by otters. I found that pike were taken very infrequently by otters in one of my study areas except during their spawning season. This may be because their habit of lying in wait for their prey amongst the water weeds, rather than swimming round after it, makes them less conspicuous to otters than some other species of fish. This protection is lost during the spawning season when the more vigorous activities of courtship bring them to the otters' attention. Similarly in Sweden, tench, which tend to be found in dense vegetation, were rarely caught.

Catchability is also the key for coastal otters. Three-quarters of the fish eaten by otters in Hans Kruuk's study area consisted of four types: eelpout, rocklings, sea scorpion and butterfish. All of these are bottom-dwelling fish and slower moving than species that live in mid-water. In fact free-swimming fish such as saithe and pollack were not commonly eaten (less than 8 per cent of the diet between them), although otters did find them a useful source of food in winter when rough seas forced them to hunt in the sheltered parts of the coast favoured by these species.

What size of fish?

There are a number of accounts of otters killing pike of 9-10 kg (20-22 lb) in weight but it seems unlikely that they would take fish much larger than these since they exceed the weight of the average male otter. At the other extreme, sticklebacks, stone loach and bullhead are occasionally taken and these may only be a few centimetres long. Usually such small prey does not form a major part of the diet but in north Norfolk, Vincent Weir once found that all the spraint he collected during one month contained stickleback remains and nothing else. It must have been worthwhile for those otters to snap up large numbers of such tiny morsels but normally the bulk of the otter's diet consists of fish between such extremes of size.

In my study area, on the edge of Dartmoor, only 7 per cent of the salmonid fish in the spraints were more than 25 cm (10 in) long and 58 per cent were less than half this length, reflecting the fact that there are a lot

Large prey may be eaten on land.

more small fish than large ones available in the river. Nevertheless very tiny fish are probably ignored unless they are particularly abundant or nothing else is available. Thus on the rivers Dee and Don in northern Scotland where otters also eat mainly salmonid fish, they take disproportionate numbers of specimens which are two or three years old (and about 12-16 cm long) compared to the more numerous but less rewarding smaller fish.

Does the diet vary through the year?
As otters tend to concentrate on the most catchable prey, and prey behaviour varies through the year, it is hardly surprising that where there is a choice, the diet varies too. In the case of fish it is activity and distribution that have the greatest effect. Eels for example tend to burrow into the mud in winter where they are hard for otters to find, so they are usually taken most frequently in the summer. More active fish such as roach and salmonids are easier to catch in the winter when the water is colder and the fish swim more slowly. Migration is also important and otters are obviously only able to feed on salmon and sea-trout while they are in the rivers. Similarly in large lakes and on the coast fish may migrate to and from the shoreline at different times of year and in both cases they are taken more frequently by otters when they are abundant near the shore.

Another activity which increases the chances of fish being taken by otters is spawning. Species that spawn in shallow water often increase dramatically in the otter's diet during the breeding season. This is particularly so for species that have limited spawning beds and gather in large concentrations, resulting in a great deal of activity which attracts the otters. No doubt the minds of the fish are concentrated on their nuptials rather than the risk of predation.

What else do they eat?
In most studies of otters' diets which cover the full year, fish make up between two-thirds and 90 per cent of the items recognized. In the few cases where fish formed less than two-thirds of the diet, otters were feeding extensively on crayfish and/or frogs as well. However, like most carnivores, otters will eat whatever they can get and a surprising array of other items has been recorded. Here, I will concentrate mainly on the significant ones.

Invertebrates: Crayfish, crabs and water beetles are the only types of invertebrate to occur regularly in otter spraint and only crayfish ever form

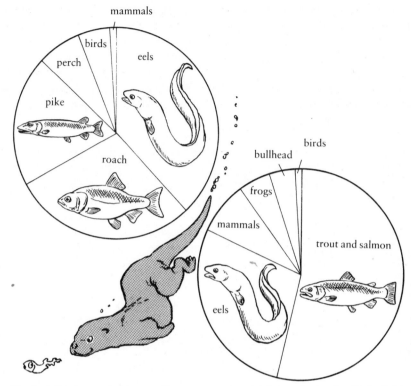

Typical diet in two habitats: a Dartmoor stream (right) *and a lowland lake* (left).

a substantial part of the diet. Interestingly, people who have studied the diet of coastal otters by looking at spraint have found that as much as 20 per cent of the diet consists of crabs. However there is an awful lot of indigestible skeleton in a crab so this may give a false picture; only 3 per cent of the captures observed by Hans Kruuk and his colleagues were of crab. Since crabs are fairly easy to recognize and only have a small amount of flesh, even this may over-emphasize their importance in the diet. Rocklings provide over four times as much energy for a given effort as do crabs, and butterfish about three times as much, so they are more worthwhile targets for an otter. Sometimes of course rocklings and butterfish may be scarce and crabs common so the otter must take what it can get; but on the whole, crabs, though easier to capture, provide a poor rate of return on the energy invested in getting them.

Crayfish also contain a lot of hard parts but they undoubtedly form a substantial part of the otter's diet in some places. On one river in Sweden their remains were found in 80 per cent of spraints collected from June to August and in parts of the River Clare system in County Galway, Eire, all scats collected during the summer contained crayfish. At all but one site in Galway crayfish contributed between 60 per cent and 85 per cent of the prey remains collected between July and December. Even so, because they have such a high proportion of shell to flesh, their contribution to the otter's nutrition must be considerably lower than this.

Amphibia: Otters living near marshy areas often consume large numbers of frogs and this seems to occur at two seasons, during hibernation and during the breeding season. At other times frogs are mainly found away from water and are much less prominent in the diet. Where frogs are reasonably common they may form as much as 20 per cent of the diet over the year but in winter and spring may reach as much as half of the items identified in some areas. Otters seem to know where frogs hibernate and search for them in those areas. During mating the

vigorous and noisy activity at the spawning sites must make it very easy for otters to find them.

Toads are hardly ever eaten. In Scotland, one study showed that of 150 spraints containing amphibian remains, only four were toads. This is not necessarily because toads are rarer than frogs but probably because they have glands in their skin which make them distasteful. Newts also seem not to be eaten by otters, but they are of course rather small and not very common.

Reptiles: In most places where people have studied the diet of otters, reptiles do not figure at all, but in one area in Italy snake remains were found in spraints, and were second only in importance to fish in the diet. I suppose a snake is much like an eel to an otter but it would be interesting to know whether they were caught on land or in the water. Some snakes hunt in water and this may make them vulnerable to otter predation. They are also fond of frogs so perhaps otters found them while both were frog-hunting.

Birds: Water-birds are the most frequent avian prey, particularly coots, moorhens and ducks. Although otters are capable of taking adult birds, predation is usually concentrated on the young and these birds tend to be taken most frequently in summer. Two surprising species in the diet in some areas are swallows and starlings. The reason for this appears to be their habit of roosting in reeds, sometimes in tens or even hundreds of thousands. Starlings do so in the winter and swallows (and martins) during their spring and autumn migrations. Whether otters catch healthy birds or simply pick up dead and dying birds as they travel through the reedbeds is not known.

Mammals: Otters would probably eat any small mammal if they could catch it but they are not well designed for hunting voles, mice and rats, so when they do occur in the diet it is probably as an incidental extra rather than the result of deliberate searching and hunting. No doubt most small mammals have been eaten at one time or another but only two species turn up more than occasionally, rabbits and water voles. Water voles probably because they live along the river bank, sometimes at quite high densities, and are therefore more likely to be encountered by otters than other small mammals. Rabbits are sizeable prey, making a good meal for an otter, and may be quite abundant although they do not necessarily live close to water. They are the one type of terrestrial (as opposed to waterside) prey it is worthwhile for otters to hunt so it is not surprising that one radio-tagged female otter in Shetland frequently ate rabbits, catching them in their burrows. I am sure many others do the same.

Carrion: There has been some debate as to whether otters feed on carrion or not. Attempts to persuade them to take bait marked with dyes or small pieces of plastic (which might show up in the faeces) have always failed – though they don't sound very tempting. However Sam Erlinge found that otters in Sweden often ate bream which had died after being caught by fishermen and thrown away and I have seen the remains of a large pike which seemed to have been consumed entirely by otters probably over a couple of days or more. Perhaps they would ignore old carrion unless very hungry, but there seems no reason why an otter would pass up the opportunity of a free meal if it presented itself.

How much do they eat?

It is virtually impossible to find this out from wild otters but in captivity male otters seem to need about 1.5 kg (3 lb) per day. This suggests that the average male otter would consume a little over half a tonne of food in a year. It seems a formidable amount! Before fishermen reach for their guns or traps, however, it is worth bearing in mind the large distances otters travel in search of their food. On an upland river containing mainly trout and salmon, they might travel several kilometres in a night and have a home range extending over tens of kilometres. On the basis of a modest-sized range on such a river, say 20 km (12 miles), a male otter would only need to find 2.5 kg (5.5 lb) per year from each 100 m (110 yd), of river. Fishermen can perhaps relax.

Eclectic tastes

One book on the carnivores suggested they will eat 'whatever they can get' and there is a great deal of truth in the notion. Some things are easier to 'get' than others for different carnivores as they are adapted to catching different prey; a hungry carnivore is likely to be less fussy about what it eats than a satiated one. On the whole, however, it is a carnivore's specialization in hunting techniques that determines the main items in its diet while chance and circumstances dictate what other items may be eaten from time to time.

It is not too surprising then to find that the whole range of food eaten by otters makes a very long list with some rather odd items in it. The strangest is a cuckoo's egg but as this was reputedly eaten by 'Tarka' in Henry Williamson's book, it may owe more to his imagination than to observation.

While eggs may not feature on the otter's menu, birds certainly do and a remarkable variety of them too. Blackbird, dipper, grouse and wagtail have been reported as well as various species of wading and swimming birds. I always thought that the small songbirds eaten by otters were taken as carrion until I read of a report in the Naturalist in 1923 of an otter catching a live sparrow. As the otter launched its attack from a distance of about 2.5 m (8 ft), it must have been a very dozy sparrow.

The remains of insects (and some other freshwater invertebrates) occur quite often in otter spraints but these usually accompany fish remains, leading to the conclusion that they were eaten by the fish which had been eaten by the otter. Water beetles do turn up in spraints in quite large numbers from time to time indicating that the otters have caught them deliberately, possibly actively searching them out. Large terrestrial insects such as dung beetles were 'greedily devoured' by some tame otters but I would never

Foraging along the strand line.

have expected the burrowing mole cricket to be at risk from otter predation. In the Doñana National Park in south-west Spain, however, it is. My Collins Guide to Insects says that mole crickets live in moist meadows, especially near rivers. This may partly explain it, but I do not know whether the otters dig for the crickets or catch them at the entrances to their burrows where they indulge in 'long periods of quiet churring' presumably for courtship purposes.

If they eat mole crickets, then why not moles? Considering their subterranean habits, moles turn up surprisingly regularly in the otter's diet, albeit at a very low level. Moles are in fact good swimmers, quite capable of crossing ditches and probably small rivers as well. They are eaten by herons too, mainly when the young disperse from their mother's range.

Slugs would be difficult to detect in spraints although the remains of earthworms have been found in stomachs of dead otters, and tame otters will certainly take slugs. However there is some dissension about whether or not otters will eat that large freshwater mollusc, the swan mussel. Most reports are based on finding the remains of a meal rather than seeing otters eat them but one person measured the distance between teeth marks on mussel shells and found that they were similar to the gap between otter canine teeth, which is suggestive if not conclusive. On the other hand captive otters seem quite unable to tackle mussels, playing with them like pebbles without opening them, although willing to eat the contents if the shells are broken for them. It may be that the mussel eating habit is passed from mother to cub, so that young otters reared in captivity which have not had the opportunity to learn that the shells contain a tasty morsel do not acquire the habit.

Otters and their prey

Many people believe that animal populations are 'controlled' by predation. Recognizing that a predator may consume large numbers of any one species of prey, they think that if it stops feeding on that species the numbers will increase uncontrollably. This is often used as justification for the introduction of another method of 'control' such as hunting, shooting or trapping. Sometimes this is indeed the case but in fact it is quite often the other way round – the abundance of the prey determines the abundance of the predator. We should not be too surprised therefore to find that although the otter used to be blamed for clearing streams of fish, especially trout, there is no evidence for this.

A few people have tried to estimate the impact of otter predation on populations of their prey and have come up with some interesting statistics. Sam Erlinge estimated the consumption of fish by otters on a lake in Sweden as being about 1,600 kg (1.5 tons) per year whereas fishermen were taking over 3,000 kg (3 tons). Fishermen took one and a half to two times as many cyprinid fish (carp family) as otters and seven to ten times as many eels and pike. Other predators included herons, grebes and mergansers, plus the fish themselves. Sam calculated that the pike in the lake probably consumed more fish than man and otters combined. In spite of all this piscivory, he concluded that the fish population in the lake could only be increased by increasing the food available, not by reducing predation.

In the stream flowing from this lake the crayfish population was also heavily exploited by otters and fishermen, and Erlinge calculated that between them they removed about half the crayfish each year, otters catching two for every three taken by fishermen. Here, too, the prey population was able to withstand the onslaught because enough crayfish grew to catchable size each year to replace those removed. Of course if the fishermen had increased their catch, perhaps by using more efficient methods of catching the crayfish, this might indeed have led to the population declining.

Hans Kruuk tried to estimate the impact of otter predation on populations of fish on the coast of Shetland. He was only able to do so for one species, the five-bearded rockling, partly because it was confined to the zone in which otters fished and partly because it was present all year round and was easily caught in his fish traps. He concluded that, on

Alert otter.

average, in each kilometre of coast there were 2,600 rocklings and each year the otters took about a quarter of these, mainly the larger specimens. Again, the population of rockings did not decline from year to year so it was clearly able to withstand this level of attack. No doubt if man suddenly discovered a penchant for five-bearded rocklings and a easy way to catch them things might be different. On a smaller scale, Hans also found that by intensive trapping he could catch all the fish in a patch of weed covering a few square metres; it would then be re-colonized within twenty-four hours.

Elsewhere in Scotland, on the rivers Dee and Don, Hans and his colleagues calculated that otters ate more than half the annual production of salmonid fish in some streams. This does not necessarily mean that they were damaging the fishing. Most of the prey were under 20 cm (8 in) in length and if otter predation were to be removed the fish might compete for food and grow more slowly or to a smaller size.

What eats otters?

As with their prey, there is still a popular notion that otters 'need' a predator to control their numbers and people often ask me what their natural predators are. Of course there are none in Britain, probably never have been.

Like other fierce carnivores, otters are well able to fight off most of the predators that live in their environment. Throughout much of their range the only predators large enough to attack them successfully would be wolves or wolverines (a larger mustelid) and there are no records of either doing so.

In general, although larger carnivorous mammals do occasionally kill and eat smaller ones, this happens very rarely. This is partly because other prey is much more abundant and also easier to subdue. It has also been suggested that carnivore flesh may be less palatable than other prey. Experiments with tame foxes showed that they would turn up their noses at weasel and badger meat even when they were hungry enough to eat voles and mice.

Otter movements and activities

Although otters are highly aquatic animals, it would be a mistake to think that they spend the bulk of their time in water. In fact coastal otters spend as much as 70 per cent of their time in their dens and even when 'active' outside their dens they spend quite a bit of time resting.

The otters radio-tracked by Jim and Rosemary Green tended to have two or three periods of activity, resting between these. The male was most energetic and spent about 60 per cent of the night on the move and 40 per cent resting. These otters left their dens around sunset and were most active in the following three to five hours. This was usually followed by another bout of activity late in the night before they settled down for the day around dawn. Occasionally they came out during the day but not very often.

This nocturnal pattern seems to be typical of otters on rivers generally but it is very different from those living on the coast, which are active during the day and hardly ever by night. It has always been believed that this was a reflection of the different levels of disturbance by humans in the two habitats but Hans Kruuk has recently suggested that this may not be so. He pointed out that the species of coastal fish eaten most frequently by otters are inactive during the daytime, hiding under stones and in weeds, and suggests that they may be easier for otters to find at this time. Maybe the otter has a better chance of catching a fish which has just been dozing than an active one. Apparently several species of freshwater fish also have periods of inactivity when they settle to the bottom and may be more vulnerable to otters. These species rest at night which may explain why inland otters are active then. On the other hand, eels are active at night and they are certainly a regular item on the otter's menu. Perhaps some species are easier to catch when they are resting (fast swimming species for example) while other, slower moving fish such as eels, are easier to catch when they are active. We still have a lot to learn.

Interestingly, otters have fairly short bouts of hunting, averaging about a quarter of an hour before they come out of the water. They then groom and rest for about the same length of time before returning to the hunt. This may be connected with their body temperatures. Despite their thick fur, otters cool down while in the water and they need to have a regular

Running up a freshwater stream.

break in which they can warm up and restore the insulating layer of air to their underfur.

As well as being active for longer periods than females, male otters travel further and a little faster, although the actual distances in both sexes vary considerably between nights and between different areas. In Sweden Sam Erlinge recorded an average distance of 9 km (5.5 miles) per night for male otters while females varied from 3 km to 7 km (2 to 4 miles) depending on whether they were accompanied by cubs and the age of the cubs. Needless to say they do not move in straight lines. Jim and Rosemary Green calculated the distances between successive daytime resting places and found that they averaged approximately 4 km (2.5 miles) for the male and 2 km (just over a mile) for the females. Actual distances travelled were considerably greater, the longest distance in one night being 16 km (10 miles) covered by the male, a remarkable feat for such a short legged animal. Even so he ended up a mere 3 km (2 miles) from his starting place.

The fastest movements were usually only recorded for short distances, for example one female managed 500 m in 10 minutes (3 km per hour/ 1.86 mph). However on one occasion, the male achieved a speed of 4.4 km per hour (2.7 mph) over a distance of 9 km although he was going downstream with a spate behind him so this record was 'current-assisted'.

Not only is there a difference in the extent and speed of movements between the sexes but also in their nature. Female otters tend to travel straight to one of a few favoured foraging areas and then move to and fro in a zig-zag pattern, presumably searching for food. Males on the other hand spend much more time in travelling and rather little in diligently searching for food, perhaps feeding while on the move. They spend much more time than the females in examining the boundaries of their ranges and make forays to every part of them. In both Scotland and Sweden it seems as though the males set off on regular patrols around their ranges, which last for four or five days.

During their travels otters use regular routes and paths. In fact in Sweden it turns out that the routes they follow when walking across the lake ice in winter are the same as the ones they swim across in the summer. They will quite frequently take short cuts across land, particularly when travelling upstream, along a particularly meandering stream or from one body of water to another. Well worn trails develop which can be quite easily recognized. They also seem to cross from one watershed to another quite readily. An otter killed on a Norfolk road, miles from the nearest river, seemed to have travelled along small brooks to a point where it had a relatively short journey to make across land between the rivers Bure and Wensum. Even so it still had to walk nearly 2 km across country to make the connection. Another Norfolk otter, released as part of the re-introduction scheme in the area, managed to find its way to an isolated gravel pit across 400 m of ploughed field.

Territory and living space

Most mammals have a fairly well defined area in which they carry out their day-to-day activities and this is known as their home range. If you track an animal over a period of time it is usually possible to work out where the normal boundaries of its range lie. It may make the occasional excursion outside them but spends most of its life in a familiar area in which it knows its way around and where to find the good feeding places and the safe dens and resting places.

Some animals actively try to exclude other members of the same species (or sometimes just the same sex) by defending their range. This is known as territoriality. Defence does not always have to be by physical aggression of course. There are many other ways of warning off intruders. Many birds and some mammals use song or other vocal calls but a much more

The evening sun on Mull.

69

subtle method is to use scent which has the great advantage of not needing the owner's presence. Rather like a sign which says 'Trespassers will be prosecuted', it gives a warning without the territory owner having to be there and, unlike singing, howling or roaring, it will last for a reasonable period of time. On the other hand scent marks do need to be backed up by at least the possibility of the intruder being caught in the act. Thus it pays territory holders to regularly patrol their territories, keeping an eye out for intruders and also making sure that the signs are still legible, i.e. renewing the scent marks.

There are many problems over territoriality, both for animals trying to implement it as a strategy and for biologists trying to study them. For example, although territorial birds can usually fly from one side of their territory to the other very quickly and see off any intruders, it is much more difficult for mammals, many of which have rather short legs in relation to the distances they may have to travel across their territory. The result of this is that intruders are more likely to get away with an incursion into a resident mammal's territory. The trespasser might be an itinerant animal 'just passing through' but it could also be a neighbouring territory holder. If some animals do intrude in this way, how can the biologist be sure that the range really is defended?

To some extent this does not matter. Although it is convenient for us to divide animals into those that are territorial and those that are not, there is no reason why the animals should fit into the neat categories we make for them or even into the same category everywhere they live. Nevertheless, people do like to organize things into neat little pigeon-holes, well I do anyway, and the fact that otters are so adaptable in their behaviour has made this one of the hardest chapters to write. If at the end you feel slightly confused about otter territoriality, please blame the otters, I feel the same.

Home range size

For most mammals the size of the range is expressed as an area but otter ranges often have to be measured as lengths, usually of river or coastline. This is a very simple and convenient way of showing how far an otter may have to travel to get from one end of its range to another but it does make comparisons difficult. For example lakes and marshes are often very important feeding areas for otters but they are best measured in terms of area. Also, measuring the length of a home range on a river takes no account of the width or depth, each of which would have significant effects on food availability.

Sam Erlinge studied home ranges in Sweden in two areas consisting of series of lakes connected by streams. He followed the otters' movements by tracking them in snow and distinguished two main categories by their footprints: males, which had large prints, and family groups, consisting of medium-sized and small footprints (medium-sized footprints on their own could have been females without cubs, or young males). Most otters had part or all of at least one lake in their ranges and all included some stream. The streams were evidently essential to the otters since in the winter the lakes freeze over and fishing is restricted to flowing water. Females with cubs had home ranges of about 6 or 7 km (4-5 miles) except for one family group which had no lake within its range and travelled along 10-12 km (6-7.5 miles) of stream. Males had much larger ranges between 10 and 20 km (6 and 12 miles) in length with an average of 15 km (nearly 10 miles).

Jim and Rosemary Green's study area, the River Earn near Perth in Scotland, had only one substantial loch in it, and their otters had much larger home ranges. The two females had ranges of 16 km and 22 km (10 and 14 miles) while the male ranged over approximately 40 km (25 miles) of river and stream. In more recent studies carried out on the rivers Dee and Don in the north of Scotland male home ranges were very variable (between 12 and 80 km/7.5 to 50 miles of river) while two females' ranges covered about 20 km (12 miles).

Coastal otters in Scotland generally have smaller ranges than those inland, typically stretching along 2 to 10 km (1-6 miles) of shore, although some exceed this and, as on inland water, males have larger ranges than females. In Shetland two female ranges which were well known included 4.7 km and 6.4 km (3 and 4 miles) of shoreline while another, where the boundaries were less well known, stretched along about 14 km (8.5 miles) of the coast. The largest known range of an animal resident in that area was of an adult male who travelled along 19.3 km (12 miles) of the coast. At the other extreme some coastal otters can find all their needs in a remarkably small area and a female tracked by Jane Twelves had a home range only 500 m (1,600 ft) in diameter. However there was probably a considerable length of shoreline within this, owing to the convoluted nature of the north-east coast of South Uist.

It is obvious that where the density of fish is high, otter ranges can be smaller and where it is low, such as on unproductive upland streams, they will need to be larger. However it is also important to bear in mind that the determining factor is not density but availability of food. Generally speaking the two things go together but there will be places and times where they do not. One such is in Sweden where the lakes freeze over in winter. If they did not, family groups could probably have much smaller territories, confined to the lakes. The need to have access to fishing areas in winter means that they must also include areas of less productive stream in their home ranges. Even in Scotland, where some otter ranges could be confined to rivers, the need to have somewhere to forage during times of spate may necessitate the inclusion of small streams and areas of marsh into home ranges. Coastal otters too must forage in times of rough seas and storms so they may need to have areas which are sheltered if parts of their range are along exposed coasts. There are also important differences in prey availability between sheltered and exposed coasts in Shetland and otters may gain further benefits by having both sheltered and exposed areas within their ranges. Rocklings and sea scorpions are found in the more exposed areas throughout the year. However if otters are to take advantage of the abundance of eelpout during the summer, they must hunt them in more sheltered spots. Likewise in the winter, the sheltered areas are good hunting grounds for pollack and saithe when exposed coasts are buffeted by the weather.

Social relationships
In Sweden most family groups had distinctly separate ranges. In one case there was a small area of overlap but generally there were gaps between the boundaries of family group ranges. This suggests that perhaps the ranges did not extend any further because all the families' needs were encompassed within them, rather than because they would encroach on a neighbour. Dog otters on the other hand had areas of overlap at the boundaries of their ranges, sometimes of 3 or 4 km. So, are they territorial?

Erlinge concluded that both males and family groups were territorial in his study area. Although the family groups did not seem to have to defend their boundaries from neighbouring families, there were never two family groups in the same range at once and other otters, apart from adult males, avoided the family ranges. Although male ranges overlapped at the edges Erlinge had two clear signs of territoriality. First, overlap *only* occurred at the edges. Second, when a resident male was shot in his study area a neighbouring male moved in and took over a substantial part of its range within a week. He also found evidence that there was a dominance hierarchy among the male otters. Those nearer the central part of his study area, which was most productive, seemed to be dominant to those in the peripheral and less productive areas. In the areas of overlap the otters avoided one another, the subordinate otter keeping out of the way or even leaving the area while the dominant one was there.

This arrangement – males and females living solitary lives and holding separate territories – is typical for members of the weasel family. They exclude members of the same sex but territories may overlap with those of one or more members of the opposite sex. However in some areas a different system prevails.

In Shetland, Hans Kruuk and his colleagues found that female otters have group territories, with up to four or five of them using the same range and respecting the same boundaries. Within this range they lead quite separate lives. They only meet infrequently and tend to avoid one another when this happens. They use separate dens and also have separate 'core areas', the regions where they spend most of their time. The territory boundaries remained stable over a period of five years despite some otters dying and being replaced. Some boundaries coincided with conspicuous features such as streams or stone walls but others occurred where there were none. Intrusions by neighbouring females were never observed, but on one occasion, when an unknown adult female encroached into a

Warning off an intruder.

territory, she was attacked by the resident. Males had much larger ranges than females and they too overlapped extensively (with other males' as well as with females'). However, male ranges did not have common boundaries and when two males met they usually fought one another. In other words, although the males did not maintain exclusive territories, the groups of females did. Why should this be?

Territories are not defended for their own sake, but for the resources contained within their boundaries. There are three resources which most animals might wish to defend and not share with others of their own kind – food, den sites and mates. In addition, freshwater pools may also be an important resource for coastal otters, not just for drinking but for washing salt from their coats after swimming in the sea. Too many otters sharing the same few pools could lead to the water becoming brackish and less effective.

On the coast, each otter needs to have sufficient lengths of sheltered and exposed coasts within its range to provide sources of food throughout the year, as well as a secure den and a year-round supply of freshwater. The coasts of Shetland are rather 'coarse grained', in that you get long stretches of exposed shores interspersed with long stretches of sheltered water. Both freshwater bathing sites and den sites are found at intervals along the coast so that otters are never more than about 700 m from either of these. However, in order to have access to all the necessary resources, a female needs to have a home range several kilometres long. Within her home range, if there is ample food and enough washing and den sites, there is no reason why she should not share with others.

A non-territorial system, with overlapping home ranges, would make it impossible to ensure that there was not too much competition for the resources. However, by teaming up into small groups and defending a common territory the females could ensure that they all had access to the various required resources but still defend them against other animals and thereby prevent over-exploitation. It would be very interesting to know whether the otters in these groups are related or not. One way such a system could develop is for young females to stay in the home range in which they were born if the resources are sufficient for sharing.

Male otters' ranges are larger then females' (much more than you would expect from the difference in their body size) and often include the ranges of more than one female and it has often been suggested that this is because it gives the male the opportunity to mate with more females than he would if he only had a range big enough to satisfy his hunger (for food). In other words the number of young produced by a male otter during his

lifetime is limited by the number of females he manages to mate with. The number of offspring produced by females on the other hand is limited by their ability to raise individual litters (which depends to a large extent on the availability of food).

Many mammals have adaptable social systems which fit in with the prevailing situation, so we should not be surprised to find that otters vary their behaviour to suit the different habitats they exploit.

Happy families in western Scotland

Not all long-term studies of otters are made by professional ecologists, and Don and Bridget MacCaskill who spent several years studying them beside a sea loch on the west coast of Scotland have also added to our knowledge. In their book On the Swirl of the Tide *they describe both the pleasures and the difficulties of trying to watch otters and learn about their behaviour.*

Some of their observations are intriguing and it would be interesting to discover whether they are a normal part of otter behaviour or unique events. For example, on one occasion, when they saw otters of two family groups playing together, one of the females left to go foraging, leaving her single cub with the second female and her two cubs. Such baby-sitting is not unknown in the carnivore family but usually occurs

in larger social groups. Could the two females have been sisters? The MacCaskills also saw an adult male otter associating with one of the families on several occasions. Once he brought a fish to the shore where it was eaten by one of the cubs which had been temporarily separated from its mother. Hardly a major contribution to the raising of the cub, but he did not avoid all contact with the family group and his supposed offspring.

The MacCaskills believed that the otters in their study area were fairly seasonal in their breeding habits, with most young born in the winter and first seen out of the den in March. One year however mating was observed in March and a litter of cubs first appeared along the shore in September, indicating a birth date in June, so they are not limited to a fixed breeding season.

Social life and behaviour

Eurasian otters are solitary by nature and probably spend more time avoiding each other's company than seeking it. Even those females that share group ranges in Shetland do not spend time in each other's company. Although the ranges of males and females overlap, there is no 'pairing' and for most of the time the sexes ignore one another. In captivity people have often kept male and female otters together without harm so there appears to be no antagonism between them but, in the wild, mutual avoidance is the norm. This changes during courtship of course and for a period of four or five days while the female is in breeding condition she will be accompanied by an escort.

Some other species of otters are much more sociable, forming pairs and family groups with both parents sharing the burden of raising the young. In giant otters and probably spotted-necked otters the young from one litter may stay with their parents after the birth of a second so that quite large groups occur. Sea otters are also sociable – at least in the sense that they can often be found in large numbers in the same place – but in this species the males and females are often found in separate groups (or 'rafts'). Each raft may number from a few dozen to several hundred, or occasionally a few thousand, individuals. Male sea otters only consort with a female when she is in breeding condition and after a period of courtship the mother is left to tackle the task of child-rearing alone.

Courting

Courtship can be an active and noisy affair. Jim and Rosemary Green were radio-tracking their male otter when he encountered a female and they described his excited behaviour over the next two nights. This included vigorous chasing through the undergrowth, rushing across a road and jumping about on a stone wall together with a great deal of chatter including purring, squeaking, grunting and even crooning. The otters seemed oblivious of the presence of an observer and even occasional passing cars. This went on for two nights and then for the following five nights the male lingered around the female's home range. However she seemed to want nothing more to do with him and after that he resumed his normal travels. Although these two otters stayed within the female's range, in Sweden Sam Erlinge followed the tracks of a courting pair which travelled a considerable distance together, covering 11 km (7 miles) of

Otters courting.

waterway, well outside the female's normal range.

The Scottish otters the Greens saw were not seen mating (although cubs arrived a couple of months later) perhaps because copulation took place in water. Captive otters have been observed mating in water as well as on land but most frequently in water. Mating lasts from 10 to 30 minutes and may occur several times during the few days the animals are together. It may be preceded by a great deal of apparently playful behaviour with the male chasing the female into and out of the water, the two otters swimming and diving together and engaging in mock fighting. Following this short period of courtship, the two animals separate and resume their solitary habits.

No doubt some of the behaviour observed between courting otters could be described as play but if, as is often supposed, courtship behaviour

is designed to give the animals a chance to ensure that both are ready for mating, it does have an extremely serious intent. Some of the activities could be interpreted as the female trying to resist the advances of the male, perhaps while she makes up her mind whether he is a suitable mate or not. The production of offspring and the survival of genes into succeeding generations is fundamentally the most important aspect of any animal's life and not to be taken lightly.

Play

Otters are renowned for their playful behaviour but, in the wild at least, it seems to be rather more rare than is generally supposed. Hans Kruuk and his colleagues observed few meetings between otters but of 84 they recorded, only 25 per cent included 'playful behaviour' while 45 per cent involved threats or avoidance. Play is certainly a common activity in captivity but of course captive otters know where the next meal is coming from and do not have to conserve their energy for important activities like foraging. In the wild play most often involves young otters which, like many small animals, indulge in a wide range of activities with no obvious, immediate purpose but which probably help them in gaining skills for life: mock fighting, mock hunting or just improving co-ordination. One young

Cubs are very playful . . .

. . . but adults rarely indulge in the wild.

otter studied by Hugh Watson had no brothers and sisters and tried instead to engage its mother in play, particularly wrestling in the water. The cub would also play on its own, rolling amongst the kelp fronds and biting at the stalks or juggling with small crabs.

Two particular misconceptions about play ought to be dispelled. The first concerns sliding. 'Play sliding' (i.e. sliding with no obvious purpose) often occurs in captivity if a suitable slope is provided but there are only a few reports from the wild and mainly for the North American river otter. Most supposed slides are simply routes into and out of the water down steep banks. North American otters also use sliding as a means of travelling over snow. They gallop along to build up speed and then launch themselves along the ground. For a short legged animal in snow this seems to be a fairly effective means of progression.

Second, there is a belief that otters will play with their prey, particularly eels, throwing them in the air and catching them repeatedly. Again, this seems to be particularly likely with captive otters, who know that if the eel escapes they will be given something else to eat instead. However it has

also been seen in the wild and it may simply be part of the otter's killing behaviour. Eels will continue to writhe for some time and the otter may simply be trying to make sure that its meal is dead before consuming it. After all, would you want to eat something that was still wriggling?

This does not mean that otters never play, but it is important to recognize that the popular image of otters as carefree playful animals does not reflect the reality of their lives in the wild.

Aggressive behaviour

There is some evidence that females may become aggressive after giving birth. In particular, one female that was studied in captivity in Sweden underwent a change in behaviour after her cubs were born. She chased and attacked the male who until that time had shared her pen for several months without any signs of aggression between them. Wild female otters in Shetland can also be aggressive to males when they have young cubs.

However, more serious aggression than the henpecking of males may occur from time to time. A Danish zoo kept two male otters in the same enclosure as a female, and no trouble ensued until they reached maturity. Eventually, the two dogs fought with each other until one escaped over a fence but not before it had been bitten in the scrotum. Don Jefferies discovered similar injuries in a road casualty and otter hunters, who would sometimes keep the baculum (penis bone) of a male otter as a trophy occasionally found that they had been fractured. Evidently otters in the wild also resort to attacking below the belt. In Shetland the most common interaction seen between adult male otters was fighting. This usually occurred on land and was brief but fierce, with the animals noisily chasing one another until one fled.

Less serious aggression also occurs and may be resolved without resort to violence. Otters with large items of food will warn off attempts to come too close with a 'yickering noise'. Usually this results in a retreat, at least until the otter in possession has finished its meal, but it does not always work and adult males have been observed stealing food from smaller animals. Similar squabbles have been observed when two otters wanted to use the same den; usually one will back down rather than risk a proper fight.

Breeding

When do otters breed?

For a long time, the answer to this question seemed to be, at any time of year. There are records of otter cubs being seen in every month in England with no apparent peak of births in any one season. The reason for this is probably that food is readily available throughout the year and English winters are not too severe. In Sweden, on the other hand, where the lakes are frozen for much of the winter and fishing is confined to the streams, there is every reason for the cubs to be born early enough to ensure that they are well grown before the severe weather returns. Hardly surprising then, that they are born in spring.

In Shetland, otters are seasonal breeders like those in Sweden; but they give birth in the summer. More than half the litters in Shetland are born in May and June and 85 per cent between May and the end of August. Here, however, it is not the severity of the weather that is important but the lack of food in winter and early spring. From January to April there are far fewer fish in the inshore area than for the rest of the year and although the fish present tend to be larger specimens, the total amount of food available is about ten times less in March and April than in July and August. Giving birth in the summer means that while the female has the heaviest drain on her needs, during lactation, food is most abundant and readily available. A little further south, in northern Scotland, otters living inland seem to produce cubs throughout the year. In mild winters this is a successful strategy but when the weather is harsh a high proportion of the litters are lost if the cubs are small.

How often?

Although otters seem to be capable of having litters in consecutive years, not all of them do. In Shetland one female failed to breed in three consecutive years whereas some bred in alternate years and others had cubs every year. It is difficult to be certain whether this variation is due to differences in the quality of the females or the quality of their home ranges. Food availability certainly plays an important part since the total number of cubs reared in a year when food was abundant was four times higher than when it was scarce. On average 60 per cent of adult females bred each year.

Where otters do not have a well defined breeding season, they have the option of having litters more than a year apart but without waiting for two full years. John Watt found that on Mull young otters stayed with their mothers a long time before becoming independent and for two females this resulted in the females having an interval of longer than a year between litters.

Gestation and birth

By studying captive animals and taking the time from the last known mating to birth, the gestation period of otters has been worked out to be close to 63 days, much the same as for other similar sized animals.

Interestingly, although several other species of otter as different in size as Asian small-clawed and giant otters have the same gestation period, the American river otter has a gestation period of eleven months because the embryo undergoes delayed implantation. This species comes into breeding condition and mates soon after giving birth in the spring. However, instead of the embryos developing normally they stop growing after a few days when they consist of little balls of cells, known as blastocysts. At this stage they would normally implant into the wall of the uterus so that they could obtain the benefit of the nutrients in the mother's blood supply. Instead they float in the uterus for several months until, two months before the cubs are due to be born, they finally implant and continue their normal development. A similar process occurs in sea otters, badgers, stoats, grey seals and roe deer as well as other species but the reasons behind it are still not fully understood. We know that in many species implantation is triggered by changes in day length because experiments with pine marten and badgers show that if you keep them under artificial light you can alter the time of implantation. In grey seals, temperature may also influence the timing of implantation. Since the length of gestation after implantation is fairly constant, using an environmental cue such as day length is a good way of ensuring that births are synchronized. However you could use similar cues to synchronize the mating period and many species of mammals do that instead.

In some cases delayed implantation may be a means to avoid mating at an inconvenient time of year. Thus, if it were not for delayed implantation badgers would have to mate in the winter when they are not very active. Grey seals mate shortly after giving birth while the females are all together on the breeding beaches instead of later in the year when they are dispersed. On the other hand these arguments do not seem to apply generally. For example common seals also have delayed implantation but they do not gather on breeding beaches like grey seals.

So although we understand the mechanisms of delayed implantation we do not have a simple explanation for it and many questions remain. Why do some species employ delayed implantation instead of mating at a different time of year? Why do American otters (and stoats) do it, but the closely related and ecologically similar Eurasian otters (and weasels) not?

Although cubs have occasionally been raised in quite public places (such as at a ferry terminal in Shetland) it is believed that otters normally give birth in more secure dens, avoiding potential disturbance. These may be on small tributaries away from a main river but it seems unlikely that the female would be too far from good feeding areas since the more time she spends travelling to feed, the longer the cubs must be left alone. Philip Wayre found that his captive females, when their cubs were due, would take a good supply of bedding (waterside plants, grass or reeds) into the den to make a substantial hollow nest, to help keep them warm while she was away feeding.

Cubs do not venture outside the den until about ten weeks old.

Litter size

This varies between 1 and 5 with 2 or 3 cubs the most common. Coastal otters seem to have smaller litters than those inland, the average produced in Shetland being about 1.8 compared to between 2.3 and 2.8 for various inland studies. Coastal otters in other areas also have smaller litters. The reasons for this difference are not at all clear but the fact that there is a consistent difference suggests that there may be some common factor. This could be connected with the ecology of the otters in different habitats but it could simply be a difference in the way the data were collected. If you calculate litter sizes from seeing the family groups when they have left the breeding den you exclude any cubs that have died in the first few weeks of life. Counts of embryos in dead otters on the other hand will not show this early mortality. Philip Wayre's records of captive otters show that the average litter size at birth is 2.4 but the average number reared to independence is 1.8 so comparisons of litter sizes from the wild also need to take into account the age of the cubs.

Growing up

Philip Wayre has watched, and filmed, the development of otter cubs inside a specially constructed breeding den, so we have a fairly comprehensive record of the growth and behaviour of captive otters during the first few weeks of life. Compared to some animals they are slow developers. At birth the cubs are tiny, about 12 cm (5 in) long and weighing between 100 and 150 g (3-5 oz). They are blind, helpless and covered with short pale fur. At this stage they suckle every few hours and make small chirruping noises but do very little else. Their eyes do not open until they are four or five weeks old, by which time they can crawl unsteadily around but not walk properly. At this age a cub will weigh 700-800 g (1.5-1.75 lb), rising to between 1 and 1.2 kg (2.2-2.6 lb) by the time it is two months old. The first solid food is taken at about seven weeks but it is another two or three weeks before they venture outside the den to play and fully three months before they first meet the medium with which they will become so familiar, water.

For animals that will eventually become so much at home in water, cubs can seem very reluctant at first. There are many stories of females encouraging or even compelling their cubs into the water but Philip Wayre has also watched cubs take to the water of their own accord the first time, simply following their mother into it. Within a few weeks the young otters

Young otter harassing its mother.

will follow the female on her travels, learning how to seek out and catch prey for themselves. Initially most of their food comes from the mother, who must make trips back to the shore with prey for them. In Shetland, young otters still only catch a fifth of their prey for themselves by January and February when they are about eight months old. Interestingly the female tends to take larger prey to her cubs than she eats herself. This is a sensible strategy since she will need to make fewer trips to the shore with large fish for the cubs than with small ones. In fact females with cubs seem to select larger fish than they do when just hunting for themselves.

The families begin to break up when the cubs are about nine months of age, although in some cases they stay with their mother until they are over a year old. Once independent, however, they have to fend for themselves, not just obtaining enough food to survive on but also finding a suitable place to settle down. Leaving home is not just a matter of bidding mother a fond farewell, it may also mean leaving behind an area that is very familiar, where the good feeding places, resting places and hiding places are well known. There may be social problems to be faced as well. Sub-adult otters in inland areas seem to live mainly in the sub-optimal, peripheral areas and if they do venture into the territories of established animals they may well have to spend much of their time looking out for the resident who may be inclined to see them off his or her territory. It is certainly a risky time and there is a higher mortality of otters in their second year of life than in subsequent ones.

The best information on dispersal of young otters comes from Idaho where a number of young American river otters were radio-tracked. In this area, where otters are not territorial, there was a variety of patterns of dispersal. Some litters of young otters stayed together for the first few months after they left home while others were solitary from the start. Some hardly moved from the areas in which they had been born while one young male travelled over 100 km (60 miles) during one month before settling down about 30 km (18 miles) from his birthplace.

Otters become sexually mature at about two years of age although in captivity one male otter of only 17 months successfully sired a litter. In the wild, females probably do not breed until they have established themselves in a suitable home range with a secure breeding den and adequate food. Young males might have to wait even longer if they need to compete with older, more experienced males, or take over a territory. Otters bred in captivity and released into the wild in East Anglia where the population was extremely low are believed to have bred at around two years of age.

Growing up on Mull

John Watt spent two years studying the development of young otters on Mull where he was able to watch them grow and gain experience at hunting for themselves. In this area, where food was less abundant than around the coast of Shetland, it was a slower process. John found that by 6 months of age young otters were still catching less than 10 per cent of their food for themselves and it wasn't until they were a year old or more that they caught all their own food.

The first attempts to forage on their own occurred at 7-8 months of age but at 12 months of age they still spent nearly half their time hunting with their mother. It was not until they were 14 months of age that they became fully independent and even then they might still be living within their mother's range. John also discovered that cubs were much less efficient at hunting than adults and, probably as a result of this, crabs (mainly shore crabs), which are easier to catch, made up about 33% of their diet even though you get comparatively little meat on a crab. This proportion decreased to about 15% by the time they were independent and to only 2-3% in adults.

How long do otters live?

A frequent and, apparently, simple question but one which is very difficult to answer. A simple answer, even if factually correct, tends to be misleading and an answer that is not misleading requires a certain amount of explanation.

A slightly different question, and one that is often at the back of people's minds is, 'How long *can* otters live?' This is simple, the answer is 'About ten years,' but misleading because only a very small proportion of otters actually live this long, probably less than 1 per cent of those born. In Shetland one female otter reached the grand old age of 10 years, while another, from Norfolk, was 9 years old when she died. However, these were only two otters out of many corpses studied. Very often people are interested in averages, 'What is the average length of life of an otter?' The answer to this, 'Probably between one and two years' is dramatically

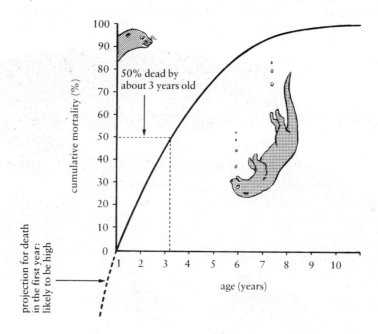

50% dead by about 3 years old

cumulative mortality (%)

projection for death in the first year: likely to be high

age (years)

Graph of mortality.

different but again obscures the true picture since many people would find it hard to envisage any animals living beyond four years if the average is less than two.

Rather than try to determine how long animals live, it is more instructive to look at when they die or, to be more precise, what proportion dies at each stage of life. In captivity, Philip Wayre showed that a quarter of cubs born died before they became independent and in the wild one would not expect the figure to be lower. A study in Canada (where trapping for fur was carried out) suggested that mortality in the first year was about one-third. In the same area half the surviving otters died in their second year of life so that only one-third of those born reached their second birthday. Once past that age the mortality was lower with only about a quarter of the survivors dying each year.

In Shetland Hans Kruuk and his colleagues concluded that their estimate of mortality in the first year of life (20 per cent) was too low partly because they could not determine mortality amongst cubs that had not left the den and also because an unknown number were washed out to sea and their bodies not recovered. They found that about 30 per cent of adults died each year.

Once they get beyond a certain age the chances of survival decrease dramatically as they begin to suffer from diseases of old age. I suspect that this happens at around eight to ten years and that is why, in the wild, few if any otters live beyond their tenth birthday. In captivity where they are cosseted, fed and attended by veterinary surgeons, otters can survive for longer, but in the real world a touch of arthritis, a few missed meals and they soon step onto the slippery slope towards starvation and death.

What do they die of?

A large number of otters die as a result of man's activities. Until about the middle of this century many were deliberately killed by trapping, shooting and hunting mainly for their fur or in the name of the preservation of fishing. More recently otters have been protected from these deaths but considerable numbers have been killed unintentionally, on the road, in fish traps and by poisoning with toxic chemicals. Otters killed on the road and in fish traps are more likely to be found than otters dying out of sight so it is impossible to know what proportion of the total mortality they represent. In Shetland about half the otter corpses recovered by Hans Kruuk and his colleagues had suffered a violent death, mainly on roads.

The Shetland otters that had died 'natural deaths' tended to be in poorer condition than the others and they also contained higher concentrations of toxic chemicals, especially mercury and PCBs. The significance of these compounds is discussed later but it is interesting to note that mercury occurs naturally in Shetland and in some older otters the concentration was high enough to cause poisoning. Most deaths by non-violent means occurred between March and June when fish were scarce and the fact that these animals tended to be in poor condition suggests that starvation might be an important factor. A similar pattern has emerged on rivers in northern Scotland where Kruuk and his colleagues found that over 40 per cent of non-violent mortality occurred in April when food was scarcest.

We have so little information on natural mortality that it is difficult to know what the most important factors are but starvation does seem very often the cause. The reason is that in order to catch its prey an otter needs to be fit and healthy. A minor disease or an injury that impedes hunting may well lead to the otter losing weight very quickly; it will soon get in a vicious circle: unable to hunt effectively because of poor condition and being in poor condition because of its inability to hunt effectively, a recipe for disaster. One otter, trapped in Cornwall by an angry farmer who had lost a goose, was in a very bad state. Meat and a goose feather in its stomach confirmed it as the guilty party but the animal had tuberculosis,

kidney stones and possible bronchitis as well as an inflamed and damaged heart and a cyst on one ureter. Had it not blundered into the trap and been shot, it seems unlikely that it would have survived much longer anyway.

Parasites and disease

Apart from the diseases recorded from this Cornish otter, two others have caused particular concern. Captive animals are susceptible to a bacterium rejoicing in the name of *Leptospira icterohaemorrhagiae*. This is carried by rats and causes Weil's disease in humans, an extremely unpleasant form of jaundice which sometimes leads to death (in man as well as otters). The only person who has looked for it in wild otters found no evidence in the fifteen specimens he examined so we do not know if it affects the wild population. Much the same is true of distemper, a disease to which a number of carnivores are susceptible but which is unrecorded in wild or captive otters in Britain although it does occur in ranch-bred mink.

Several parasites have been found in the guts of otters, including spiny-headed worms, roundworms and tapeworms; in one sample of otters from Shetland, half were parasitized. Most of the parasites found infect various predators of fish but one species of tapeworm was specific to otters and the spiny-headed worm species mainly parasitizes seals.

Otters do not seem to suffer much from external parasites although they occasionally carry ticks. Neither ticks nor fleas seem to mind a semi-aquatic existence because they are often found on mink and it may be that they would be more common on otters were it not for their dense coats.

Many parasites are very particular about the species of animal they will live on and there is one species of louse that is only found on the Eurasian otter. Its name, *Lutridia exilis*, reflects this, but it is far from common and has only been recorded ten times since its first discovery in 1815, including three times in Britain (in 1919, 1930 and most recently in 1987). It is very small (about 1.2 mm long) so it could easily be missed and as few people spend their time looking for lice on otters the rarity of finds is perhaps not surprising. Even so, up to 150 otter corpses have been carefully searched by Nature Conservancy Council scientists over a period of nearly thirty years and only one, from the Island of Lewis, had lice, and this was the animal with the most recently recorded specimens of *Lutridia exilis*. On the other hand, I have seen one otter that was crawling with ticks although she was somewhat emaciated and in very poor condition. This particular animal was also blind, a condition which seems to be more common in otters than one might expect. James Williams, a naturalist in Somerset with a keen interest in otters, collected together twenty-two records of blind otters, most of which had lost the sight of both eyes. Some of these were in poor condition, but ten were described as being in good condition so they were presumably still able to hunt. They came from a wide area in Britain although most were from the south and there were no records prior to 1957, despite attempts to find one. Since otter hunters were keen diarists and often recorded peculiarities of the animals they killed, James concluded that blindness was a new phenomenon, but did not try to explain it. People have suggested that it might be caused by one of the herbicides which is often used on the road-side and can affect the cornea, but this would be difficult to prove.

Predation

As pointed out earlier, there are no natural predators of otters in Britain or in much of the rest of their range either. The most common 'predator' of otters is probably the motor car, however there are a number of records of otters being killed, though not eaten, by domestic dogs.

Are otters pests?

Much of the rest of this book is concerned with the relationship between man and the otter which, until quite recently, has always been a rather one-sided affair with the otter on the losing side; first we persecuted them, then we poisoned them; now at long last we are trying to protect them.

Originally persecution was carried out in the name of preservation of otters' prey. In the sixteenth century they were regarded as serious pests and a bounty was placed on their heads because of attacks on fish ponds and fish traps. At that time they were either trapped or hunted with hounds and in some areas there were local laws requiring fishermen to keep a dog for hunting otters. Fish were an important source of protein and competition with the otter was not to be tolerated. It is quite impossible now to judge whether otters really did reduce the food available to man but in well stocked fish ponds they could have been a major problem: concentration of prey makes for good hunting.

As time went on, more sophisticated methods of killing came into use. By the end of the eighteenth century, firearms were more reliable and useful for dealing with vermin. During the nineteenth century the development of the well keepered sporting estate ensured that predatory mammals and birds had a hard time in the face of guns and traps, particularly the gin trap. Wildcat, polecat and pine marten all suffered under this onslaught and were driven back to small areas in Wales and Scotland although the otter survived throughout much of its range.

During the twentieth century the number of keepers declined dramatically, especially after the First World War and in the last few decades both the polecat and pine marten have begun to spread back into parts of their former range. Even so, eagles, peregrines and kites are still being poisoned, trapped and shot in the name of 'game preservation', although this is now illegal. Despite the lack of evidence that predators seriously affect the populations of their prey, many landowners and their keepers would rather not take the risk even if it means breaking the law. The old attitudes still prevail in some areas.

What about otters, are they still pests? Well, it is not many years since I listened to a Member of Parliament declare that he was not going to have otters attacking his salmon and he would make sure that the keepers on his Scottish estate (where otters were not at the time protected) would continue to control them. At about the same time there was a great deal of

fuss being made in one part of the west of Scotland where otters were reported to be killing sheep. It was claimed that a total of 82 were killed over a period of 7 years including full grown sheep as well as lambs.

On the whole the evidence against otters is pretty thin. Like the medieval monk who relied heavily on intensively 'farmed' fish in monastic fishponds, the modern fish farmer could suffer enormous damage to his well stocked ponds or nets. Hundreds or thousands of fish are packed into very small areas and fed on a highly nutritious diet to fatten them up for the table. A paradise for otters. Although there are complaints about the attentions of otters, they have not reached the proportions one would expect from the proliferation of such farms, particularly in Scotland. This is because in the areas where there is a high density of otters and of fish farms, in the lochs and sea lochs of western Scotland, the fish are maintained in netted enclosures from which it is relatively easy to exclude otters. Fish farms on rivers are more vulnerable, as are artificially stocked fisheries, although many of these are in areas where otters are scarce and those at risk can minimize the chances of damage by using suitable fencing. One sensible recommendation is to keep a guard dog. This may put off otters and will certainly deter human predators.

Despite the concerns of the MP and many other keen fishermen, natural populations, whether of game or coarse fish, are unlikely to be significantly reduced by predation. Although in theory each salmon taken by an otter is one less for the fisherman, in practice other factors such as the impact of salmon netting and pollution have a far greater effect.

Similar arguments apply to predation on waterfowl. Otters are only likely to be a potential problem when ducks are maintained artificially at a high density. On the whole, mink are more likely to cause problems for people who keep large collections of waterfowl although otters are not entirely free from blame. During the 1930s an otterproof fence was put around some lakes in Shropshire in order to establish a duck farm. Unfortunately there was an otter on the inside of the fence which managed to eat its way through £600 worth of ducks before it was caught!

The supposed attacks on sheep do not stand up to close examination either but there are occasional reports of otters eating lambs. Quite often they are implicated because kills occurred near water or the lambs were killed in a manner *supposedly* characteristic of otters. On the whole however, if this does occur, it seems to be so rare that compared to natural mortality at or shortly after birth, otters can hardly be considered a significant problem.

Hunting otters

Otters have been hunted by man since time immemorial, initially just for their fur, later to protect fish stocks and more recently for pleasure. Even hunting with hounds goes back at least 800 years. There was a King's Otter Hunt in 1175 when Henry II was monarch and the regal interest continued through the reigns of King John (who was very fond of his otterhounds), Edward II (who had a pack but spent more of his time hunting deer), Henry IV who maintained a 'valet of our otterhounds' and Henry VIII who also kept a pack of otterhounds. It seems pretty clear that the main motive for otter hunting was pleasure but, although it was sometimes quite fashionable, it was generally seen as a lesser sport than hunting 'noble' quarry such as deer or even foxes. Hunting otters with dogs for sport has always been a mainly British pastime, though it was not confined to Britain and in the 1930s there was a pack based in central France (Monsieur Guyot's Otterhounds).

There is a great deal of hunting literature and a surprising number of books devoted to the histories of individual otter hunts. Even today, more than ten years after hunting ceased in Britain, people still collect these books and one or two new ones have recently been published. They make interesting reading. Otter hunters had a great respect for the otter and in some of the older books long chases are recorded with great relish. Otters that gave a good chase were held in esteem. In a book about the history of the Dartmoor Otterhounds one otter which eluded the hounds for nearly two and a half hours before being finally killed was described as 'the hero of the day'. An otter which had provided such a good chase might be allowed to go free, presumably in the hope that it would provide another good day's sport on a later hunt. Conversely otters which succumbed rapidly were often regarded as rather feeble creatures. At the same time, while many people enjoyed the thrill of the chase, not all looked forward to the kill and many people went hunting because it was the only way they could be sure of seeing otters.

During a hunt the hounds would first 'draw' the river, searching for the scent or 'drag' of the otter. Once found this had to be traced to where the animal was lying up, a feat requiring some skill on the part of the huntsman to ensure that the hounds followed the trail towards it rather than away. When the otter was located, either seen escaping or tracked to a den or burrow, it was recorded as a 'find'. If it did not try to escape,

Otterhound.

perhaps because it was in a secure den, attempts would be made to bolt it using terriers, poles or even spades. The hounds were held back until the otter had a chance to get away ('given law') and were then allowed to set off in pursuit. As each pack consisted of 20 to 30 hounds, one might expect that the otter would have little or no chance of escape from such formidable 'predators' but, although dogs can travel much faster on land, they cannot swim as fast as otters, nor can they dive. On the other hand they can run along the bank to keep up with the otter and stickles were formed by hunt followers to turn the otter back towards the hounds. Once the otter was amongst the hounds its chances of escape were much lower, especially as, if it did slip away, people on the bank would be looking out for it. Some otters got away through their own devices, while others were allowed to escape by the huntsman. Hounds on their own (even in a pack) would probably not be able to catch many otters but with human help they could kill up to three-quarters of those found, though half was more usual.

The otterhound

When otters were still reasonably numerous throughout Britain there were over a dozen packs of hounds maintained specifically for hunting them. Many of these packs contained a mixture of breeds, with English and Welsh foxhounds predominating, but two packs, the Dumfriesshire and the Kendal and District Otterhounds, had packs of pure-bred otterhounds with pedigrees stretching back into the nineteenth century. It is clear that hunts commonly carried out judicious cross-breeding to improve the strain in their packs so it is not surprising to find the origin of the otterhound itself in a cross – between a bloodhound and rough-coated French hound (the Griffon Vendean). The result is best described as looking like a long-haired bloodhound and it was particularly noted for its stamina,

its voice and its very keen nose, all pre-requisites for a successful otter-hunting hound.

The total population of pure otterhounds was never very high because only two hunts had pure-bred packs while others had a few otterhounds together in their mixed breed packs. When the otter population declined to the level at which legal protection became inevitable and otter hunting ceased, there was some risk that the extinction of the otterhound was imminent. However some of the packs were kept on for hunting mink (and still do so today, nearly fifteen years later), while the master of the Kendal and District Otterhounds decided that in order to maintain the breed it should be registered with the Kennel Club and bred for show rather than for hunting.

If this sounds a bit tough on the otters, just bear in mind that until the mid to late nineteenth century nets were used to ensnare them and barbed spears to impale them, methods that were considered quite barbaric by twentieth-century otter hunters. Indeed in the later stages of otter hunting when otters became very scarce and the object became to find rather than to kill them, the stickle too was abandoned.

Like most sportsmen the hunters claimed that they were able to control the numbers of otters and prevent them reducing fish populations. However they also maintained, particularly in the last few years of hunting, that they were keen to preserve otters. This might appear a paradox, but I suspect that there is more truth in the conservation role – at least in the nineteenth century – than in the argument about controlling numbers. I have a strong suspicion that one of the reasons the otter did not suffer the fate of polecat, pine marten and wildcat in the last century was because, like foxes, they were beasts of the chase. Landowners and river keepers could be persuaded to leave the 'control' of otters to the hunt rather than taking it into their own hands. The fact that hunting was less effective than shooting and trapping and that the hunts had a vested interest in making sure that there were otters left to hunt next year was conveniently overlooked, or at least accepted in return either for compensation for damage or the opportunity to take part in hunting. Incidentally is it very interesting to find that the mink hunts, most of which have been formed since otter hunting ceased, stress the 'control' argument while the otter hunts, towards the end, stressed the 'preservation' argument. Nevertheless despite their stated aim of preserving their quarry during the second half of the twentieth century, otter hunts were quite powerless to prevent the population from declining in the face of modern threats to its well-being even though they changed from trying to kill otters to trying to count them.

One effect of the decline in otters was a reduction in the numbers of hunts and also the frequency of hunting. In 1951 there were 12 active hunts which between them hunted for 571 days finding 395 otters. In 1961, 11 hunts achieved 584 days hunting and found 314 otters. However by 1971 the same number of hunts was only out on 371 days finding 181 otters and by 1976 there were only 9 hunts who found 86 otters in 215 days. 1977 was the last year in which otter hunting took place in England and Wales because the following year the otter was protected under the Conservation of Wild Creatures and Wild Plants Act. Several of the old otter hunts turned to hunting mink, some disbanded and one concentrated on ensuring the survival of the otterhound as a breed.

Otters have also been hunted for their fur, and in many European countries where the fur trade is well established most otter hunting has been for this purpose, using traps and to a lesser extent guns. The luxuriant fur has long been popular and otters have probably suffered for this ever since man first learnt to sew skins together. In the fifteenth century, their pelts were used as a form of currency – John, son of Dermod, had to stump up 164 otter skins in lieu of rent owed to Henry IV and as early as the fourteenth century there are records of otter skins being imported to Britain from the Continent. Even in the 1960s and 1970s otters were being trapped for their skins in parts of Scotland; at that time they were worth about £10-£15 each.

In other European countries substantial numbers were killed, about

1,000 per year in Sweden during the 1940s and 1950s and 200 per year in Denmark. Even during the 1970s, 600 were being killed each year in Norway. The greatest numbers however came from Russia where between 4,000 and 8,000 were killed annually from 1940 to 1970, although in the early 1970s the numbers were considerably lower and hunting was banned in at least one region. Despite these culls, it seems unlikely that killing otters for their fur or for sport has been responsible for the declines that have taken place in most European countries. This is not the case for other species of otter, however. The sea otter nearly became extinct in the second half of the nineteenth century mainly because its habits made it much easier to find and kill. The giant otter has suffered a similar fate in some parts of its range during the twentieth century and once more its habits may make it more vulnerable to hunters. Giant otters are more sociable than Eurasian otters, living in large (and sometimes quite noisy) family groups which are active by day, and are also quite inquisitive. It's also possible that the indigenous people of South America are more effective hunters than those in Europe.

Decline and fall

It was in August 1962 that an article, written by Jack Ivester Lloyd, appeared in the magazine *Gamekeeper and Countryside*. It was entitled 'Where are the Otters?' and the author, a keen hunter himself, explained that the otter hunts had found very few otters over the past few seasons. He speculated on the reasons for this and concluded that over-zealous river clearance was at least partly to blame, in particular the removal of bankside trees, osier clumps and reedbeds, perhaps combined with excessive water extraction leading to lower water-levels. Another hunter suggested that too much disturbance by fishermen, picnickers and bathers had driven the otters away.

This lack of otters clearly worried the hunts and from that time on there was a policy of reducing the number killed during hunting. Before 1960 about half the otters that were 'found' by hounds were killed but that proportion declined steadily during the 1960s till by 1970 it was less than 15 per cent and did not exceed that level while hunting continued. By the 1970s the policy was to kill only those thought to be injured or diseased or if strongly urged to do so by a landowner suffering damage. If you bear in mind that fewer otters were being found at that time anyway, it is not too surprising to find that the average kill in the 1970s was only 11 per year over the whole country.

The scientific community also became concerned but was not able to produce tangible results quickly. It was not until 1969 that the report of a sub-committee of the Mammal Society was published which confirmed fears that numbers of otters had declined seriously, especially in the south. The authors of this report found it very difficult to obtain firm evidence of a decline from the 160 individuals and 20 river authorities which responded to requests for information. Although many people believed that there had been a decline they could not provide data to back this up. In contrast, the otter hunts were able to pass on records of the numbers of days they had been out hunting and the numbers of otters they had found and killed.

As the hunts did not all spend the same amount of time hunting each year, the figures were converted to a proportion which indicated the number of otters found per hundred days hunting so that they could be compared. There was quite a lot of variation between different hunts and different years but in the years 1900, 1937, 1947 and 1957 the average success rate was between 64 and 80 otters per hundred days hunting, with the average in 1957 being 72. However, in 1967 the average was 44 otters per hundred days with all the hunts but one showing a decline since 1957. The authors concluded that the decline had taken place, or at least started, between 1957 and 1967, but could not pinpoint the date more accurately. It was nearly ten more years before we could get any closer to the exact timing and causes of the decline.

The report suggested six factors which might have caused the decline: the severe winter of 1962/63; pesticides; increase in fishing; increases in tourism and pleasure boating; trapping for fur; destruction of habitat; but could not determine which, if any was the most important. In 1977, the report of the 'Joint Otter Group' (see p.118) added to these a further five pressures on the otter which had also been suggested as causes of the decline: hunting; disease; road casualties; the spread of mink; protection of fisheries. Again, it was not possible to determine the significance of any of these.

During 1977 I moved to Cornwall and met a keen hunter who showed me copies of the *Yearbook of Otterhunting* dating back to 1950. Although he did not have a complete set, another acquaintance from Northumberland also had an incomplete set and between the two I was able to piece together the records for all the otter hunts from 1950 to 1966. The Mammal Society's first report had figures for 1967 and a second one published five years later took the records up to 1971. Using these data it was possible to pinpoint the start of the decline much more closely and with the help of Don Jefferies of the Nature Conservancy Council I could show that it must have started round 1957 in much of southern Britain. This date, together with the fact that the decline was more or less simultaneous over a wide area but most serious in the south, enabled us to reject many of the suggested causes of the decline and we came to the conclusion that the introduction of a new kind of insecticide (dieldrin and related compounds) was responsible. Many birds and mammals were killed by these chemicals when they were first used and there were dramatic declines in the populations of some birds of prey such as peregrine falcons and sparrowhawks.

Dieldrin, and related compounds such as aldrin and heptachlor were first used in 1955 for a variety of purposes. A particularly important one was as seed dressing for cereals but they were also used for sheep dipping, in the woollen industry, for moth-proofing carpets and blankets, and for timber treatment. They are extremely effective pesticides but are very persistent and continue to act for a long time. Unfortunately they are

poisonous to birds and mammals as well as to insects.

Some animals were poisoned directly, mainly by feeding on dressed seeds. Huge numbers of finches and small songbirds died, as well as many woodpigeons, although fewer tears were shed over these. Other animals, the carnivorous species, received their poison second-hand by feeding on the seed-eaters. Many peregrine falcons, barn owls, sparrowhawks and foxes were killed in this way. The insecticides soon found their way into the rivers, leaching through the soil as run-off from fields or as waste from sheep dip. Once there they were absorbed by tiny micro-organisms in the water and the concentrations built up to a higher level in the fish which fed on them. From there it is a short step to the fish-eating birds, such as herons and grebes, and mammals, like the otter, and with each step in the food chain, the concentration of chemicals in the body increased.

In the end the predators may have died of poisoning. Although there are no records of otters being found dead of pesticide poisoning during the 1950s and '60s (the first case was recorded in 1972) both foxes and badgers were found dead and dying from this secondary poisoning as were many birds of prey. The lack of dead otters is no surprise when you consider how scarce they are compared to foxes and badgers which also live and forage in areas where their bodies are far more likely to be spotted. Unfortunately, even if otters were not killed outright, the population could still have suffered from the effects of sublethal poisoning. Once the pollutants reach a critical level they begin to affect the physiology of the animals. In particular the reproductive system can be affected, resulting in a variety of problems, from unusual behaviour, such as egg smashing in birds, to sterility. Significantly there were reports of fewer badger and otter cubs being seen during the late 1950s and early 1960s. Indeed this was even mentioned in Jack Ivester Lloyd's original article.

From 1962 onwards there were a series of bans on the use of dieldrin and similar compounds: first their use was banned for spring sown cereal, then for various other seed dressings, for sheep dip in 1966 and for autumn and winter sown cereals in 1975. By the late 1970s few agricultural uses remained and the large numbers of birds and animals killed by these chemicals were a thing of the past. Peregrine falcon and sparrowhawk populations recovered in numbers but sadly the recovery of the otter population has been slower and in some areas it has continued to decline in the 1980s. The reasons for this are not entirely clear and probably vary from place to place. Disturbance by humans and habitat destruction are commonly considered to be the most important and we shall look at those in more detail later. First we shall take a brief aside to look at the relationship between mink and otters and at the ways in which otter populations are assessed now that otter hunting has ceased.

Otters and mink

It must be a hard life being a mink. Just about everyone seems to hate them. I have been fascinated by them for many years but I despair of persuading more than a few fellow admirers that this charming little creature is a welcome addition to Britain's mammalian fauna. 'Vicious killers', 'bloodthirsty brutes', 'savage invaders': the epithets rain down on this attractive furry animal rather smaller than the average cat. Mink first arrived in Britain in the late 1920s, brought by fur farmers who bred them for their luxuriant fur. Small numbers probably escaped from the start but it was not until the mid to late 1950s that they started breeding in the wild and brought down the wrath of the British public on their heads, just because they killed some poultry and a few fish.

I am not going to defend the mink at great length here but I do want to consider one accusation, that it has been in some way responsible for the decline of the otter. The reasons for this allegation are quite straight-forward – that over much of Britain, and at several localities in particular, there was a remarkably short period of time between the arrival of mink and the disappearance of otters. The fact that in many places the otter disappeared *before* mink arrived tends to go unnoticed, not least because otters tend not to leave a sign saying 'Gone away' when they become extinct.

Taking Britain as a whole, the start of the decline of the otter was in the mid to late '50s, exactly the same as the start of the spread of mink. This was an extraordinary piece of bad timing on the part of the mink, which should have had the good sense to wait for another ten years or so before starting to conquer Britain. Even so, the otter's decline occurred simultaneously over much of the country, but at the time mink were confined to a few rivers in just three or four counties. Further evidence against the linking of the mink's spread with the otter's demise is provided by recent surveys which show that in two of the areas where mink have been established longest (south-west Wales and south-west England) the otter populations are doing best.

Although the evidence for mink driving out otters is very weak, it is worth looking in a bit more detail at the accusations. The least credible I have heard is that otters do not like the smell of mink. I can well understand this, having occasionally felt the full force of the mink's scent glands which it occasionally discharges when upset by being caught in a trap. However mink do not smell any better or worse than other carnivores such as badgers, foxes, weasels, or even otters, except when they are frightened. The smelliest British carnivore is probably the polecat (it used to be known as the 'foumart', short for foul marten) and otters have been sharing their ranges with polecats for thousands of years without trouble so I find it hard to believe that a few smelly mink would displace them.

Apart from this there seem to be four main accusations: 1. that mink compete with otters for food; 2. that they aggressively drive otters out; 3. that they carry diseases which could spread to otters; 4. that they kill otter cubs.

Competition for food is in many ways the most interesting and, superficially at least, the most likely. The diet of mink is very similar to otters in the range of prey although there are considerable differences in emphasis. While otters concentrate on food caught in water, mink are much more likely to take prey from beside water or even on land. Over a wide range of habitats the proportion of fish to birds to mammals in the mink's diet is approximately equal, with frogs forming an important item in a few areas. Mink are the jacks of all trades of British carnivores, their diet overlapping to some extent with many of the native species but, like proverbial jacks of all trades, they are masters of none. Otters are better at catching fish, polecats better at rabbiting and hunting birds, and stoats and weasels are superior ratters, mousers and hunters of voles.

Feral mink.

The mink's secret weapon?

As far as the otter is concerned, competition could occur for fish, which form from 20-55 per cent of the mink's diet and 60-90 per cent of the otter's. However otters are much better at catching fish than mink and should have little difficulty in out-competing them. It is important to bear in mind that competition occurs when something is in short supply; if there is plenty to go round there is no problem. In Sweden, when otters are confined to fishing on streams in the winter because the lakes are frozen, it is the mink which moves away to the smaller, less productive areas, not the otters.

Such 'scramble' competition is only one form of interaction between two species with similar diets. Another is known as 'interference'. In this case, one species, usually the larger, makes sure it does not have to share the food supply by using threats or physical violence. Could mink, the largest of which weigh no more than 1.3 kg (3 lb) really drive out otters, when even otter females weigh 5 kg (11 lb) or more? I doubt it, especially when you bear in mind the fact that otters occasionally eat mink. The much quoted viciousness of mink is no greater than you would expect from a carnivore of this size. Predators need to be fierce to kill their prey, which may be as large as, or even larger than, themselves. Stoats and weasels have even more ferocity per ounce than mink, and otters are capable of inflicting much more serious damage because of their larger size.

The possibility of mink carrying a disease which might spread to the otter population cannot be lightly dismissed. In particular, canine distemper has often been mentioned, not least because it occurred in mink on fur farms. More recently, a dead otter from Norfolk had symptoms similar to those of Aleutian disease, another virus which affected ranched mink. Apart from these, rather tenuous, connections there is no evidence that otters in Britain have suffered from the outbreak of an infectious disease. Given the numbers of otter corpses that have been examined over the past thirty years, it seems likely that if there was a problem it would have been noticed.

The story of mink killing otter cubs is an old one but it is difficult to find a reliable first hand account. I have heard a number of stories of small brown bodies being carried by mink and in most cases these could as easily be rats or water voles as otter cubs. The most reliable report I have seen was from someone who saw a mink carrying a partly eaten otter cub and found another dead cub in a hollow tree nearby. Although the mink was not seen killing the cubs this is the nearest we have to evidence that it happens. Even so, mink are much smaller than adult otters which might be expected to guard their young fiercely and I feel that it is most unlikely that this is a serious problem.

There was a suggestion at one time that even if mink were not responsible for the original decline of the otter, perhaps their presence would stop it from recovering again. Happily there is good evidence from Devon to show that this is not so, despite the fact that we have had mink breeding wild in Devon for over thirty years. The otter population crashed here as elsewhere but in the last ten years there has been a recovery and otters are once more to be found on rivers from which they were absent in the 1970s. On balance, there is little doubt that the creature that has had the greatest effect on otter populations is man and there is little to be gained by trying to transfer some of the blame to the mink.

Otter surveys

When otter hunting in England and Wales came to an end in 1977 the statistical records of hunting effort and finds ceased as well. However, by that time each hunt was, on average, only active for 24 days per season and the average number of otters found per hunt per season was 9. This meant that it was becoming difficult to make comparisons between hunts or years because the sizes of the samples were so small. Large apparent changes from one season to the next could be due to chance rather than to changes in the population. It was also apparent that some hunts increasingly concentrated their efforts on rivers where they had a good chance of finding otters and hunted less where they knew they were absent, thereby inevitably biassing the results.

Other methods of monitoring otters began: in 1976, the Otter Survey of Wales started, followed in 1977 by surveys in England and Scotland and in 1980 by the Irish survey. Prior to that time there had been a number of smaller scale surveys carried out by volunteers. These included whole counties such as Norfolk and Suffolk, river systems such as the Tweed and various others in different parts of Britain. All gave valuable information but because of the patchy nature of observations it was difficult to build up a picture of the situation in Britain as a whole. Comparisons were difficult because people used different methods of surveying and had different levels of experience. The national surveys overcame these problems by employing and training full-time surveyors who searched in a fixed pattern, putting the same amount of effort into each area and river system.

The technique involved selecting a series of sites along each river between 5 and 8 km apart. At each site 600 m of bank was searched for signs of otters (usually spraints) and a sheet was filled in, recording the type of river and whether or not signs were found. In Scotland and Wales the whole country was searched in this way but in England, where only one surveyor was employed, the country was divided up into 50 km squares, using the national grid, and alternate ones were searched. During these 4 surveys nearly 11,000 sites were fully surveyed and signs of otters were found at 54 per cent of them. However there were some major differences between the four countries and also within each country (see table and maps).

The greatest contrast is between England and Ireland, with otters being

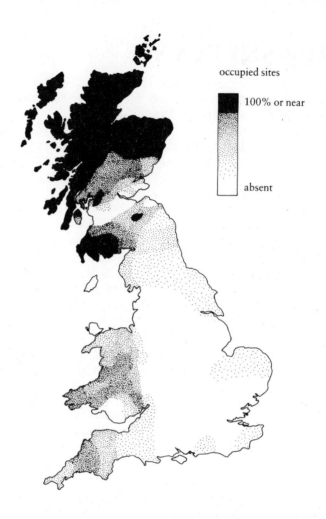

occupied sites

100% or near

absent

Distribution of the otter in Britain in the 1980s.

restricted to very few parts of England (signs found at 6 per cent of sites) while being found more or less everywhere in Ireland (92 per cent of sites). In Scotland otters were widespread (73 per cent of sites) but fewer signs were found in the south, particularly between the Firth of Tay, the Southern Uplands and the Firth of Clyde. This is the most populated area of Scotland and is also heavily cultivated. In Wales, signs were most common in the south-west and on the Severn catchment but were much scarcer in the south and east, with none in the Glamorgan area or Gwent, apart from a solitary spraint near Cardiff.

In England, apart from the south-west and the Welsh borders, signs were very hard to find indeed. There were small concentrations in Northumberland and north Norfolk but elsewhere signs were scarce or absent.

These studies were repeated seven years after the original surveys, with very interesting results. In Scotland only the southern and eastern halves of the country were re-surveyed and here there was a small but encouraging increase in the percentage of sites where signs were found (from 57 per cent to 65 per cent). In Wales there was also an increase, from 20 per cent to 38 per cent which was spread over much of the country. The south-west (Dyfed) remained a stronghold as did the Severn catchment but signs had increased substantially on the Wye. Glamorgan remained fairly otter-free, however, and the surveyors were disappointed to find that otters had become extinct on Anglesey.

In England too there was an increase (from 6 per cent to 9 per cent) and, as in Wales, some areas did better than previously, while others did worse. The Welsh borders fared well with a doubling of sites with signs on the River Wye and a more modest increase in the upper reaches of the Severn. The south-west also showed a substantial increase from 24 per cent to 44 per cent. The bad news however came from East Anglia where the proportion of sites with signs decreased from 20 per cent to 8 per cent. In several places where signs were found they were close to areas where otters had been released as part of the Otter Trust's re-introduction programme (see later) and may therefore have been produced by these animals.

There are plans to repeat these surveys at intervals so that we can continue to keep a check on the status of the otter in Britain. The third Welsh survey was finished in 1991, resulting in a further increase in the number of sites with signs of otters (52 per cent of those searched), particularly in South Wales. The third English and Scottish surveys also started in 1991 and will be completed during 1993. Similar surveys, using the same technique, although often on a smaller scale, have now been carried out in a number of European countries, as well as North Africa and the Near East. The method provides a simple repeatable 'snapshot' of the otter situation which can give an initial impression of the distribution of otters in a country.

The greatest value of these surveys is in making comparisons, either between different areas or different times, but it is extremely important to take care in the interpretation of the results and a certain amount of controversy has been generated about it. It would be very nice if there was a direct relationship between the results of surveys and numbers of otters, a doubling in the percentage of sites with signs representing a doubling of the otter population. This is unlikely to be true. It is even more difficult when you compare different areas, some places have more suitable sprainting sites than others and not every 600 m stretch of every river with otters will have signs within it. On the other hand if you search about 100 sites in an area 50 km square (as was done in the English survey) and find no signs of otters in any of them, it is reasonable to reach the conclusion that otters are scarce or absent there. While in an area in which 90 per cent or more of the sites have signs, it would be reasonable to conclude that otters were widespread although it would not necessarily mean that the numbers there were as high as they could be.

The difficulty has occurred where people have tried to use spraint density within sites as an indicator of the size or 'health' of the otter population and, as explained on p.22, this is not really possible. It is certainly true that where otters are known to be common, spraint is much more abundant than in areas where they are known to be present but very scarce. However even in one area the density of spraint varies through the year so comparisons made between areas searched at different seasons would be meaningless. In Shetland, where the density of otters is well known, it was impossible to find any relationship between the density of otters and the density of spraint.

Shetland is the only place where it has been possible to estimate reliably the actual population of otters. Here, otters only use a few dens each and in an intensively studied area, Hans Kruuk and his colleagues found a close relationship between the number of well used dens and the number of adult female otters (3 dens per female). They also knew that adult females formed 55 per cent of the otters in the area. Following a den survey over a much wider area they were able to calculate that there were between 700 and 900 adult otters in the whole of Shetland.

Current threats

The start of the initial decline of the otter in Britain can be pinpointed to the 1950s, but there is now abundant evidence that although the population is still widespread in some areas it has continued to decline elsewhere. For example, the two surveys of England demonstrate that otters were found in a much smaller area of Norfolk in 1985 than 1978. Similarly a series of studies on the Somerset Levels shows that the area inhabited by otters there steadily decreased between the early 1970s and the early 1980s. If dieldrin and related pesticides were the only factors affecting otter populations, one might have expected a widespread recovery. After all, peregrine falcon and sparrowhawk populations have increased substantially and the concentrations of pesticides in their bodies and eggs have declined since the 1960s. Evidently, there is more to the decline of the otter than the pesticide problem. The subsequent history of otter populations in Britain, particularly the differences between areas, has undoubtedly been influenced by other factors.

Over the last 10 or 15 years, many people have tried to pin down the factors that have been most important in limiting populations. Several have been considered and many of them have been shown to affect otters. Chris Mason and Sheila Macdonald from the University of Essex have been especially active in this field yet in their book they could not point to one particular factor. Instead they concluded that different combinations of factors in different areas were probably responsible for local declines or failures to recover.

Habitat destruction
The worst period for otter habitat damage probably occurred in the 1970s and early 1980s following the formation of ten large water authorities from the smaller river authorities. Many of the newly formed authorities embarked on substantial programmes of river 'improvement', most of which were to the detriment of otters. The wholesale removal of bankside trees must have led to the loss of many den sites while the clearance of scrub and reedbeds, drainage of wetlands and the straightening of rivers to improve drainage all took their toll of lying up and feeding areas. During the 1980s the authorities became much more mindful of the needs of otters and other forms of wildlife but there are still calls for improving drainage of areas which would, if left, form valuable otter habitat, and if

Where disturbance is low otters may take a nap in the open.

removed, simply add to the problems of overproduction of some agricultural products within the European Community. I have been fascinated to discover that since privatization and in a more environmentally aware era the water companies have become even more conscious of the need to be nice to otters although I have an ungenerous suspicion that the benefit to their images is a significant consideration in this.

Disturbance

Observations of radio-tracked otters suggest that they may be more tolerant of human disturbance than was once thought. They have been followed as they have swum past small groups of people and solitary fishermen and have remained within their dens despite the obvious presence of human activity, including banging in fence posts and cutting down bankside vegetation and felling trees nearby. Only when the workers were directly overhead did the animals move. Some otters have used dens very close to regular human activities including one near a cafeteria (with outdoor tables) in Scotland while a number of litters of cubs have been raised in a den beneath a busy jetty at the Sullom Voe Oil Terminal in Shetland.

I recently watched an otter in the village of Craighouse in the Hebrides where the road runs along the shoreline. It was busy tucking into a large fish and apparently oblivious of a dog walking along the road a mere 30 m away, not to mention two men mending their car at the roadside and five biologists training a battery of binocular, telescope and camera lenses upon it.

Two other pressures which need to be taken into account are accidental deaths and pollution, both of which, perhaps in association with habitat destruction, can lead to fragmentation of populations, in itself a serious problem for otter conservation.

Accidental deaths
The numbers of otters killed inadvertently by man may be a significant drain on the population in some areas although, of course, most casualties occur where otters are most abundant. For example over half of the 113 corpses collected by Hans Kruuk and his colleagues on Shetland suffered violent deaths and of these, 48 were road casualties. In the Outer Hebrides Jane Twelves found that otters are not infrequently killed on the small, island roads. More serious however is the fact that there are some accident black spots for otters in areas where they are scarce, for example, five were killed in a seven-year period on a small river in north Norfolk. They all died at a place where the river ran under the road and was blocked by a sluice gate at certain times. When this happened otters would cross the road, occasionally with fatal results. I have also heard of places in south-west England and Wales where a number have been killed at the same spot.

A second, and equally worrying form of mortality occurs when otters are caught in fish traps and crab or lobster pots. Again, large numbers

may die in relatively small areas where otters are common. Jane Twelves recorded 23 otters drowing in fyke nets set for eels in the Outer Hebrides during 18 months in 1975-6. Records of a further 23 killed in the same way in freshwater were collected by Don Jefferies and Jim and Rosemary Green over a period of many years but 8 of these were killed in Norfolk during the 1970s including 6 in one year. A substantial blow to such a small, fragmented population.

Lobster traps also take their toll. Jane Twelves recorded 22 otters killed off South Uist in the 3 seasons from 1978-81 and otters are regularly drowned in Orkney, Shetland, Skye and Sutherland.

Toxic chemicals
Despite the restriction on using dieldrin, DDT and other organochlorine pesticides over the years, they are still present in the environment. This is partly because some are still used but also because they persist for many years before being broken down. In addition to the few legitimate uses, there are suspicions that some compounds are still being used in non-approved ways and occasionally the compounds 'escape' into the environment. One such escape occurred on the River Tone in Somerset during the 1970s when washings from a woollen mill were released into the river. Another happened a few years later, in Devon, when a contractor dug into a dump containing dieldrin causing considerable leakage. Dieldrin was later found in fish and otter spraints downstream of the site.

Other pollutants may also have an impact. The damaging effects of the presence of PCBs (polychlorinated biphenyl compounds) in the environment was not realized until some time after the problems with pesticides were being dealt with. PCBs are used in a number of manufacturing processes and occur in such diverse products as plastics, lubricants and brake linings. They are similar to organochlorine insecticides in some ways: their persistence, their solubility in fat and the fact that they are toxic if they occur in high concentrations in animal tissues. For example they can cause sterility in mink if they reach about 50 parts per million in some tissues. Concentrations well above this have been recorded in the fat of otters from parts of Sweden.

Heavy metals such as cadmium, mercury and lead have also been found in the tissues of otters, again sometimes at levels which could lead to poisoning. People have also expressed concern that other forms of pollution such as acid rain might affect the otters by reducing or removing their food supply. Two types of pollutant which might be beneficial to otters in small quantities are sewage and the run-off from agricultural fertilizers such as nitrates. In modest quantities these enrich the water, leading to increased production of fish, which would be to the otters' advantage. However higher concentrations lead to over-enrichment which can result in the oxygen supply being used up and the fish dying, leaving the otters with no food.

One further risk, to coastal otters this time, is oil pollution. In an incident in Shetland in 1978, at least thirteen otters were killed when oil was spilled into the sea, but sea otters are at even greater risk. When the *Exxon Valdez* ran aground in Alaska in 1989, it led to the deaths of large numbers of sea otters in the vicinity.

Fragmentation

Otters are much less mobile than birds and, when populations are low, and perhaps scattered, the apparently minor effect of a small number of casualties whether from natural causes, road deaths or from drowning in fish traps can have a dramatic effect on the chances of recovery. Two female otters died in 1984 on the rivers Glaven and Stiffkey in north Norfolk and a third in 1986, after which there were no further signs of otters on either river. One otter was old (nine years) the others younger. As the nearest other known otters were many miles away, that small population was evidently doomed to extinction and with their deaths otters disappeared from another part of their remaining range in East Anglia. The results of the England otter survey suggest that there are other places where similar situations may exist.

Food supply

The radio-tracking studies carried out in Scotland by Hans Kruuk and his colleagues suggest strongly that human disturbance and possibly habitat destruction are not as detrimental to otters as was once thought. Their research shows that in northern Scotland at least, the amount of food available has a strong influence on the distribution of otter activity and on otter mortality. It may be that the same is true elsewhere in Britain and that lack of food has been partly responsible for changes in otter populations and distribution. As yet we have no evidence to go on. Efforts to record changes in fish abundance have been frustrated by lack of historical records for the type of fish eaten by otters. Now that we have more information on the abundance of fish in areas where otters still live it would be very instructive to make comparisons with areas from which they have disappeared.

Conservation

Given all these problems facing the otter, it is hardly surprising that a great deal of thought and effort has gone into otter conservation over the past fifteen years or so. This has involved a wide range of activities from campaigning and lobbying Parliament to heaping up tree trunks and digging holes in the ground, all of which have, in their different ways, made a contribution.

Things really began to happen in 1976 when the Friends of the Earth Otter Campaign was initiated by Angela King, Angela Potter and John Ottoway. At about the same time, the Society for the Promotion of Nature Conservation (now the Royal Society for Nature Conservation) joined with the Nature Conservancy Council and other bodies to form the Joint Otter Group (affectionately known as JOG). One of the main aims of the FoE campaign was to get the otter protected by law (under the Conservation of Wild Creatures and Wild Plants Act). JOG's task was to find out what was known about the status of otters, establish what other information was needed and to consider what measures should be taken (if necessary) to conserve otters. JOG agreed with Friends of the Earth (and many other people) that otters ought to be protected but was advised that it was not possible under the Conservation of Wild Creatures and Wild Plants Act. Fortunately the Department of the Environment was persuaded to change its mind shortly after the first JOG report was published. Legal protection for the otter was debated in Parliament during 1977 and approved by a small majority so that by January 1978 the otter was protected in England and Wales.

What was it protected from? Well, mainly from people catching it and killing it (or even attempting to catch or kill it). This meant the end of otter hunting in England and Wales; although the hunts were not trying to kill otters at that time, there was a risk that an otter might be killed accidentally or that hunting might be interpreted as an attempt to catch one. Also I suspect the hunts realized that chasing a protected animal was a bad policy, even though, at the time, they believed that the extent of the decline had been overstated. JOG did not conclude that hunting or killing otters was the reason for their low numbers so some people questioned

By the late 1970s, otters in England were largely confined to well wooded rivers and streams in north and west Devon.

whether legal protection was necessary or desirable. 'Why protect an animal from something that did not appear to threaten it?' My own view is that it was desirable. Not so much for what it prevented but because it made it quite clear that the otter was an endangered species and in need of special protection. This had a powerful educational effect when it came to persuading other people to do things for the benefit of the otter, a protected species.

When a few years later the Wildlife and Countryside Act came into force, protection for the otter was strengthened. Otters are now protected in Scotland as well as England and Wales and the new act makes it an offence to disturb or destroy their dens, a powerful weapon in the protection of the otter's habitat as well as the species itself.

To back up the educational effect of legal protection, it was also important to explain to people the best ways to help conserve otters and their habitat. The Otter Trust and the Otter Haven Project were both concerned about this. The trust, with its captive otters and well designed displays was able to gain the attention of a wide spectrum of the public. The project concentrated particularly on riparian owners and water authorities and produced a booklet with guidelines on practical management of waterways which catered for the needs of wildlife as well as flood prevention, sewage disposal and water supply.

Both organizations encouraged and helped the setting up of otter havens. These were first proposed in 1975 when the Nature Conservancy Council and the Anglian Water Authority convened a small group to advise on otter conservation in East Anglia. Havens were originally envisaged as relatively small areas along rivers where the otter's needs would be particularly catered for. Disturbance would be minimized and the growth of suitable bankside vegetation and preservation of trees encouraged. As time went on the idea developed further with practical work being undertaken to improve the habitat: stretches of bank were fenced from stock to allow scrub to develop; trees were planted and also thickets of scrub species; 'stick piles' were created from waterborne branches or tree trunks to provide lying up places; in some areas artificial dens were built from drainpipes and bricks.

As this was going on, much time was spent liaising with water authorities and landowners to try and prevent further loss of good otter habitat. Surveys were organized to find important places for otters, particularly potential dens and lying up places so that they could be left when management took place. By the end of the 1980s water authorities in many areas were commissioning surveys to identify sites of conservation importance (for all forms of wildlife) before carrying out extensive management.

Efforts were also being made to reduce other threats to otters. In one or two areas, otter underpasses were set up to try and alleviate the risk of road deaths. The effectiveness of these is almost impossible to judge, partly because otter deaths were not common, even in the worst areas, and partly because they were placed in areas where populations were already fragmented and low. A research project on eel fyke nets demonstrated that a carefully designed guard could prevent otters getting into the net without seriously depleting the catch and it was recommended that these should be used by fishermen.

Reducing pollution is of concern to everyone and, although much research has been done on the distribution and effects of the pollutants, finding ways of reducing them is much more difficult. The creation of the National Rivers Authority as an independent organization responsible for water quality may have a significant effect on pollution since previously water authorites were responsible for adding to pollution (mainly from sewage works) as well as preventing it.

A final weapon in the conservationist's armoury is re-introduction. Seen by most people as a last resort, it is still of potential benefit and it is of course important to make sure that, if it is done at all, it is done effectively. This is why the Nature Conservancy Council worked with the Otter Trust in carrying out a pilot re-introduction programme in East Anglia. The otters were bred in captivity by the Otter Trust. Several were released in groups of three, one male plus two females, while others were released as pairs. Prior to release, when they were about 18 months old, the groups were placed in a large, quiet enclosure, away from public display. In due course they were taken to the sites chosen for release and kept in small enclosures for two or three weeks. Eventually a gate was opened and the otters allowed to leave. Food was provided for the following twelve days, but less was put out each day. In some of the groups, one animal, usually the male, was provided with a radio-transmitter which enabled the researchers to see how his home range developed. By the end of 1989, 18 otters had been released in this way in East Anglia.

The programme did demonstrate the feasibility of releasing captive-bred otters and it was found that they tended to stay in the area selected for them. Within a matter of a few weeks they were using home ranges in a similar way to otters tracked on Scottish rivers. There is also indirect evidence that they have bred successfully and the Otter Trust believes that there may now be second-generation otters in the area.

We now know that captive-born otters can be successfully released into the wild. The next question to consider is when and where this should be done. Many people feel very strongly that it should only be a last resort, perhaps to bolster a small and fragmented population, such as in East Anglia. Even then one has to question why the population is small and fragmented. There is little point in releasing captive-bred animals unless they have a good chance of survival. Similarly, it would be unwise to release otters in areas where the wild population is expanding (such as the Welsh borders and the south-west). The release of captive-bred animals may well have a part to play in the conservation of otters in Britain but it is important that they should be released as part of a carefully prepared plan which should be rigorously monitored.

What can you do?

Well please don't ring or write asking for a couple of otters to release on your local stream. As you can see, it is quite a complicated business and not always advisable. If you do own the banks of a river or a stream which you want to improve for otters and other wildlife, contact the Royal Society for Nature Conservation's Rivers and Otters Project for advice. Apart from this, it is very difficult for individuals to do a great deal on their own but it is always worthwhile supporting your local Naturalists' Trust in its efforts to protect local wildlife. Any help you can give, whether by joining, fund-raising or giving practical help is always welcome. The only national organization concerned with otters is the Otter Trust whose address is given below. Other conservation organizations which actively protect and conserve wetlands (such as the RSPB) are of great benefit to otters as well.

Otters in literature

Many people were first introduced to the otter as Ratty's friend in The Wind in the Willows. *I certainly was.* The Wind in the Willows *was published in 1908 and it seems unlikely that Grahame's anthropomorphic descriptions of animals had much effect on the public perception of the real animal at that time or since. However, nineteen years later Henry Williamson published* Tarka the Otter *which, I am sure, has been much more influential. Far from* writing about otters as if they were little people, Williamson tried to write a story about otters, based on his impression of their actual way of life. He described their daily lives and activities as active predators feeding on fish, frogs and rabbits and also recounted in some detail the deaths of otters as they were shot at, trapped and hunted by man.

Many admire Williamson as a writer but I must confess that I have never really enjoyed Tarka and it did not encourage me to read his other books. For those who do appreciate him, part of the appeal seems to lie in Williamson's descriptions of the north Devon countryside. If you know the area you can follow Tarka's travels very accurately because Williamson describes real places. I have even swum in the Junction Pool near Tarka's 'birthplace' (and found numerous signs of real otter activity there as well).

In recent year's Tarka has been recruited into the tourist industry with British Rail naming their delightful route linking Barnstaple with Exeter as 'The Tarka Line' and Devon County Council devising a 'Tarka Trail'. The trail consists of a network of footpaths (some 180 miles of them) around the river valleys of the Taw and Torridge, along the North Devon coast and up onto the hills of Exmoor. All areas which 'Tarka'

(i.e. Williamson) knew well.

However, the book that first brought otters to the attention of a wide audience was Gavin Maxwell's Ring of Bright Water published in 1960. I can still remember hearing extracts read from it, possibly on the radio, or at school. Over 100,000 copies of the book were sold in its first year of publication and it became a bestseller in America as well as in Britain. In 1962 a children's version, The Otter's Tale, was published and my own copy of this was my first introduction to 'real' otters. Ring of Bright Water was published as a Penguin paperback in 1974 and eventually made into a film as well. I have no doubt that its portrayal of otters as lovable, playful creatures influenced many people's views of this animal which, only a few years earlier, had been regarded as enough of a pest to warrant control by hunting.

Some people, particularly in the hunting fraternity, criticize the book saying that it persuaded many people that otters make suitable pets. They certainly come over as endearing animals but if you read it carefully, you can see that they are also very demanding and cannot be kept in a conventional home.

Maxwell's two subsequent books, The Rocks Remain and Raven Seek Thy Brother show how his apparently idyllic lifestyle on the west coast of Scotland came nearer to tragedy in subsequent years. Otters continued to feature largely in his life, despite the loss of Mijbil, his first otter, which strayed from home and was killed by a workman. These books reveal more fully the difficulties of keeping wild animals as pets. Even in his remote corner of Scotland with no neighbours Maxwell had to create zoo-like conditions to maintain his otters. He also discovered the unpredictability of wild creatures in captivity when two of his otters made serious attacks on people. The result of one of these was that one of his assistants had two fingers amputated. In the end he tried, unsuccessfully, to place the otters in suitable animal collections. Maxwell's story is a complex and fascinating tale but one moral is clear – otters do not make good pets.

Further information

Reading

Otters: Ecology and Conservation by Chris Mason and Sheila Macdonald (Cambridge University Press, Cambridge, 1986). An excellent account of the biology of the Eurasian otter with a strong emphasis on conservation. A little dated.

The Natural History of Otters by Paul Chanin (Croom Helm/Academic Press, London, 1985). Attempts to review the biology of all species of otters. Slightly more dated.

The Track of the Wild Otter by Hugh Miles (Elm Tree Books, London, 1984). An account of his efforts to film otters in the wild. Beautifully illustrated, with many interesting observations. The film of the same name is also worth looking out for in case it is repeated.

Otter Spraint Analysis by Jean Webb (Mammal Society, 1976: new, extended edition due shortly). For those who want to get down to basics.

Sea Otters by John Love (Whittet Books, London, 1990). Will encourage you to plan your holidays on the coast of California (or possibly Alaska).

The Handbook of British Mammals, edited by Gordon Corbet and Stephen Harris (3rd edition. Blackwell Scientific Publications, Oxford, 1991). The first edition inspired my original interest in mammals. The latest one is a mine of information about British mammals.

The Encyclopaedia of Mammals, edited by David Macdonald (George Allen and Unwin, London, 1984). If the 'Handbook' does not inspire you, then this will. A richly illustrated and comprehensive account of the world's mammals.

On the Swirl of the Tide, by B. MacCaskill (Jonathan Cape, London, 1992). A summary of twelve years of otter watching on the Scottish coast.

Addresses

The Otter Trust, Earsham, Bungay, Suffolk

The Mammal Society, Conservation Office, Zoology Department, University of Bristol, Woodland Rd, Bristol BS8 1UG

Your local County Naturalists' Trust (or Wildlife Trust) should be in your phone book or you can contact the parent body:
The Royal Society for Nature Conservation, The Green, Witham Park, Waterside South, Lincoln

Index

References in **bold** indicate illustrations

If you have enjoyed this book, you might be interested to know about other titles in our **British Natural History** series:

BADGERS
by Michael Clark
with illustrations by the author

BATS
by Phil Richardson
with illustrations by Guy Troughton

DEER
by Norma Chapman
with illustrations by Diana Brown

EAGLES
by John A. Love
with illustrations by the author

FALCONS
by Andrew Village
with illustrations by Darren Rees

FROGS AND TOADS
by Trevor Beebee
with illustrations by Guy Troughton

GARDEN CREEPY-CRAWLIES
by Michael Chinery
with illustrations by Guy Troughton

HEDGEHOGS
by Pat Morris
with illustrations by Guy Troughton

OWLS
by Chris Mead
with illustrations by Guy Troughton

POND LIFE
by Trevor Beebee
with illustrations by Phil Egerton

PUFFINS
by Kenny Taylor
with illustrations by John Cox

RABBITS AND HARES
by Anne McBride
with illustrations by Guy Troughton

ROBINS
by Chris Mead
with illustrations by Kevin Baker

SEALS
by Sheila Anderson
with illustrations by Guy Troughton

SNAKES AND LIZARDS
by Tom Langton
with illustrations by Denys Ovenden

SQUIRRELS
by Jessica Holm
with illustrations by Guy Troughton

STOATS AND WEASELS
by Paddy Sleeman
with illustrations by Guy Troughton

URBAN FOXES
by Stephen Harris
with illustrations by Guy Troughton

WHALES
by Peter Evans
with illustrations by Euan Dunn

WILDCATS
by Mike Tomkies
with illustrations by Denys Ovenden

Each title is priced at £7.99 at time of going to press. If you wish to order a copy or copies, please send a cheque, adding £1 for post and packing, to Whittet Books Ltd, 18 Anley Road, London W14 0BY. For a free catalogue, send s.a.e. to this address.